Boston Red Sox · 100 Years · The Official Retrospective

EDITED BY KEN LEIKER, ALAN SCHWARZ AND MARK VANCIL

DESIGNED AND PRODUCED BY: Rare Air Media
1711 N. Paulina, Suite 311, Chicago, Ill. 60622

PUBLISHED BY: Vulcan Sports Media, DBA The Sporting News
10176 Corporate Square Drive, Suite 200, St. Louis, Mo. 63132

TEXT BY: Edited by Ken Leiker, Alan Schwarz and Mark Vancil
Copyright © 2001 by Rare Air Media. Produced in partnership with and
licensed by Major League Baseball Properties, Inc.

First Edition
Library of Congress Cataloging-in-Publication Data
is available from the Publisher.
ISBN 0-89204-677-5
99 00 01 02 RA 10 9 8 7 6 5 4 3 2 1

RARE AIR BOOKS
A DIVISION OF RARE AIR MEDIA

ACKNOWLEDGEMENTS

Style might lord over substance and conscious introspection often yields to conditioned response, but there remain instances when uncommon kindness and character push through the cultural clouds to shine for all to see. We talk about these people because they touch a part of us buried beneath the day-to-day business of life. When we think about them, there is a quality to our memory. In the end, they are people who warm the moments and smooth the bumps. For this stretch of track, they extended from Boston to Atlanta to Chicago to New York and points in between. They are:

Ken Leiker, a friend and colleague, whose talent and character are self-evident. He never wavered despite the most unreasonable request and never once answered a problem with anything other than a solution.

Not surprisingly, Alan Schwarz came to us from Ken. Like Ken, Alan's ability and professionalism is matched only by his desire to achieve perfection — on deadline. Much of this book was born in Alan's mind and its quality, particularly in the writing, is a direct result of his efforts.

At the Boston Red Sox, Larry Cancro and Debbie Matson are the kind of gentle souls we all might hope to become. Kind and considerate despite a challenging life of his own, Larry calmly guided us through Red Sox history while making us feel as like a member of his family. Meanwhile, Debbie was simply as kind, warm and caring as anyone you could hope to meet at church much less in business. Dick Bresciani plowed through page after page despite ringing phones, appointments and more than a quarter century full of memories. If Dick saw it, then he remembered details not even the combatants could hope to summon. Indeed, every person that touched this project on behalf of the Red Sox was nothing less than kind and giving including Jeff Goldenberg and Rick Subrizio.

Steve Buckley and Jerry Crasnick are old friends whose ability and kindness were essential to this book. The work of Allen St. John was equally important and the late-inning efforts of Herb Crehan and David Scott closed some last-minute holes.

Among the many pleasures born of this process was working with Ken Shouler, whose persistence was of particular importance in the Title Years chapter.

Though we met and exchanged thoughts almost exclusively through email, Steve Marantz's effort on the 1967 season was essential to the integrity of the entire project. He wrote with passion and grace, providing context to a defining year in the lives of many New Englanders.

At The Sporting News, the reconnection with Steve Meyerhoff and our introduction to Kathy Kinkeade made the entire effort worthwhile. Steve's combination of integrity and talent always made writing for The Sporting News a wonderful experience. He brings those same attributes to books. Kathy has the kind of mind and passion that the larger book publishing community would do well to study. The effort and intellect of TSN's Dave Weiner, who drove this book through the sales channels, Ron Smith and Joe Hoppel were also necessary and much appreciated.

At Major League Baseball, Don Hintze remains a committed business partner and friend. This book would not have happened without Don's considerable input, passion and trust. The sports publishing business is better with Don as one of its leaders.

At Rare Air Books/Rare Air Media, the efforts of Frank Fochetta and John Vieceli, my partners and friends, continue to make life and business a seamless and joyful exercise. Steve Polacek, Nick Lo Bue and Nick De Carlo's work on the graphic design of this book is obvious and enduring. In yet another schedule that would have reduced the project to a fire drill for lesser talents, Steve, Nick, Sr. and Nick, Jr. turned out excellence by working late into the night and all through weekends without complaint. In the words of their spiritual leader, "You can't teach that." The fingerprints of Dave Durochik, who once again captained our photography search, Melinda Fry, Dennis Carlson, Shannon Mounts, Andy Pipitone and Paul Sheridan, our counselor and conscience, can be found throughout the finished product as well.

As always, the support, love and gentleness of my wife, Laura Sadovi-Vancil, and our girls — Alexandra, Samantha and Isabella Rose, whose beauty graced the world during the creation of this book — remain gifts beyond any expectation.

Mark Vancil - 2001

THE BREARLEY COLLECTION

Dennis Brearley walked his guests up the stairs of his studio and offered his chair. No matter where you looked history seemed to look back in the form of the famous and infamous, but always from a print of a beautiful photograph. The Brearley Collection is one of the great photography collections in all of sports, one that Dennis, Sr. and his family, sons Matt and Dennis, Jr., and wife Susan, make available to thousands of fans across the country through a catalog and retail shop at Boston's Faneuil Hall. But what they have is secondary to who they are. The Brearleys opened their studio and photo files at a moment's notice and worked all weekend to provide us with images necessary to complete this book. If you have never seen the Brearley Collection, go to Brearley.com or visit the Brearley Collection shop at Faneuil Hall the next time you're in Boston. With any luck, you will have the pleasure of meeting one of the Brearleys along the way.

SPECIAL THANKS

David Durochik at Sportpics, Michael Bacino at Corbis, Prem Kalliat at Sports Illustrated, Elvis Brathwaite at AP/Wide World Photos, Mario Prosperino at AllSport, Bill Burdick at The Hall of Fame, Vince Llamzon, Pete Knipschield and the staff at Professional Graphics, Sara Vadgama and the rest of the Butler and Tanner team.

PHOTOGRAPHY

AP/Wide World Photos	85, 103, 108, 109, 121, 148, 149	John Riley, *AP/WIDE WORLD*	61
Archive Photos	114	Herb Scharfman, *SPORTS ILLUSTRATED*	175
John Bazemore, *AP/WIDE WORLD*	60	David Seelig, *ALLSPORT*	59
Boston Red Sox	14	Sports Illustrated	56, 62-63
Paul Chiasson, *AP/WIDE WORLD*	64	Rick Stewart, *ALLSPORT*	35
Brearley Collection	29, 66, 152-153, 174, 175	Winslow Townson, *AP/WIDE WORLD*	60
Corbis	32, 34, 35, 36, 40, 42, 43, 69, 70, 71, 72, 74, 75, 76, 80, 81, 82, 83, 84, 85, 87, 88, 89, 90, 91, 95, 96, 97, 98, 99, 100, 104, 105, 108, 109, 110, 113, 115, 116, 117, 118, 120, 122, 123, 124, 125, 127, 132, 134, 136, 138, 140, 141, 143, 145, 146, 150, 151, 153, 154, 157-65, 167, 168, 169, 172, 174, 175	John Williamson, *MAJOR LEAGUE BASEBALL*	51
		John Zimmerman, *SPORTS ILLUSTRATED*	155
		PHOTO RESEARCH BY SPORTPICS:	
		AP/Wide World Photos	35, 109, 158
		Scott Boehm, *SPORTFOLIO*	58
James Drake, *SPORTS ILLUSTRATED*	35	David Durochik, *SPORTPICS*	4, 6-7, 14, 15, 16, 21, 22, 26, 27
Otto Greule, *ALLSPORT*	35, 39, 50	Kathleen Economou	64-65
Hall Of Fame	8, 12 , 13, 14, 15, 18, 128, 131, 133, 136, 137, 138, 143	Ric Fogel, *SPORTFOLIO*	52, 68
		Tony Inzerillo	66
Walter Iooss, Jr.	1, 10, 11, 16, 17, 24, 25, 30, 33, 35, 48, 73, 75, 92, 93, 106	Louis A. Raynor, *SPORTSCROME*	81
		Bruce L. Schwartzman, *SPORTPICS*	176
Walter Iooss, Jr., *SPORTS ILLUSTRATED*	35, 41, 79	Sports Imagery Inc.	60, 61
Fred Kaplan, *SPORTS ILLUSTRATED*	38	Transcendental Graphics	2-3, 16, 44, 68, 81, 119, 129, 130, 132, 139, 142, 156, 172, 174-176
Heinz Kluetmeier, *SPORTS ILLUSTRATED*	173		
Phil Long, *AP/WIDE WORLD*	55	Robert Tringali, *SPORTSCROME*	6-7, 10, 16, 20, 21, 57, 171
Doug Pensinger, *ALLSPORT*	61	Ron Vesely, *SPORTPICS*	72, 76, 78, 176
Rich Pilling, *MAJOR LEAGUE BASEBALL*	25, 26, 27, 35, 46, 47	Bryan Yablonsky, *SPORTSCROME*	56
Art Rickerby, *TIMEPIX*	94, 107	Michael Zito, *SPORTSCROME*	54, 170

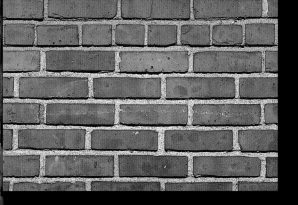

CONTENTS

The Green Monster

THE MOST FAMOUS FENCE IN THE MAJORS

THE GREEN MONSTER

It is a movie screen of memories, a flat expanse towering over Fenway Park with decade upon decade of the grand old ballpark's charm and history projected onto it. Gaze at the Green Monster and then close your eyes — the plain background slowly morphs into images of Ted and Yaz and Dewey and Wade and Nomar, their swings and their gazes up to the Wall. The most famous fence in the major leagues — indeed, the most identifiable feature of any American sporting venue — might as well be a seashell, with its memories recorded inside and played back forever.

Every now and then Nomar Garciaparra will walk out to the Wall before batting practice to see the history imprinted by countless line drives slamming against it over the years. "It looks like a golf ball — it has all these dents from all these balls hitting it," Garciaparra says with a boyish bounce. "Now when I see it, I think, 'I know I have a dent in there somewhere.' And you think of all the great players who have a dent. You look up there and it's a history of baseball. It's almost like a signature: Rice. Yastrzemski. A million names, all these great players. And I have one. Who am I next to? And who's next to me?"

Fenway Park, the oldest stadium in major league baseball, stands sentry over the sport's traditional past with its brick facade, obstructed-view seats and, more than anything, its unique outfield wall. Forced to conform to city streets and trolley lines as all stadiums once were, Fenway's fence has more nooks and crannies than an English muffin — 17 faces in all, each with 17 dozen stories to tell about some poor outfielder bumbling around out there.

"It's not often that a center fielder can go straight to his left and slam into a wall," Paul Molitor says. For all its twists and turns the best part of the fence is the 9,000 square feet of flat nothingness looming over left field. "I was always afraid," Bill Lee once said, "that it would fall down and kill Rico Petrocelli at short."

The Monster has been called dreamy by hitters, confounding by fielders, and words that can not be reprinted here by pitchers. John Updike called it "a compromise between Man's Euclidean determinations and Nature's beguiling irregularities." Even the distance of the Wall from home plate, once listed at 315 feet, is a mystery. A skeptical Boston Globe reporter sneaked into the park

"...a compromise between Man's Euclidean determinations and Nature's beguiling irregularities."

JOHN UPDIKE

WIDTH
231'

SCREEN
23'

HEIGHT
37'2"

FOUNDATION
22'

Take The
Gillette
SensorExcel
Challenge

Bett
Wea
Bau
Disp

VS

379
115.

THE PROFILE OF A
GREEN MONSTER

a few years ago, measured the distance, and claimed it was more like 305 feet. The official distance now reads 310. The Monster stands 37 feet, 2 inches high, and extends 231 feet long, its foundation sinking 22 feet below ground and its screen extending 23 feet above the wall — with the ubiquitous CITGO sign beyond it as the cherry on top.

With baseball careening into the 21st century, tradition is vulnerable. Venerable old ballparks such as Tiger Stadium have been abandoned for modern, feature-filled facilities built for the contemporary industry. Fenway is no different — a new one probably will be on the scene by decade's end. But the Wall will survive, either replanted or replicated in the new place as a nod to the Red Sox's long history. And you can be sure it will continue to be painted the same Fenway Green presented by nearby Wilmington painter Ken Smith and approved by owner Tom Yawkey in 1947 and still

provided today by his son, John. "The Monster is the first thing people think of," Garciaparra says. "Even people who don't know baseball, when they hear of Fenway Park they go, 'Is that the one with the big green wall?' There's so much history here. I love it."

Fenway's left-field legend began the day the park was opened in April 1912. Though a 25-foot fence stood almost exactly where the Monster does today, the wall didn't capture people's attention as much as the precarious embankment in front of it. Quickly known as "Duffy's Cliff," for Red Sox left fielder Duffy Lewis' mastery at negotiating the 10-foot incline, scurrying up and down it like a gloved gazelle, the embankment was as famous in its time as the Green Monster is today. Lewis, who would pinch-hit for a rookie named George Herman Ruth in Ruth's first game, July 11, 1914, succeeded where many others failed; a successor named Smead Jolley once tumbled down the

SHERM FELLER

In Boston, there have been two voices louder than those of any other in the entire metropolitan area — nay, all of New England. This notion is as tried and true as Legal Seafood's New England Clam Chowder, Boston Baked Beans and The Tea Party and will always and forever be so, with no room for discussion.

For the beloved Boston Celtics it was the gravelly, smoke-filled lungs of the late Johnny Most.

And for Red Sox Nation, it was the deliberate, distinguished tones of the local institution, Sherm Feller. As the Boston Globe's Bob Ryan wrote after Feller's death in 1994 at the age of 75: "Central Casting just called. They regret to say they will not be sending over any more Sherm Fellers. ...He

embankment on his rear end and joked, "They taught me how to run up the cliff, but they never taught me how to run down it." It took less than a year for Duffy's Cliff to become, like the Wall did later, a part of Red Sox strategy. The Boston Post wrote during that first season:

If the Red Sox should win the pennant by a margin of two or three games — which is entirely possible — there will be no doubt that that bank made the difference...

It is sodded at an angle of forty-five degrees. To catch a ball running up this bank, or to run for one so that one can keep his equilibrium when he strikes the bank, requires study and practice.

When Lewis first saw the bank he realized that it was up to him to get the balls that went there, so he has practiced daily all season when the Red Sox were at home playing balls that are driven to the bank or against the fence. Nearly every game played at Fenway Park since then has

given the spectators a chance to see Lewis dash for the bank, grab a fly ball in one hand and fall part way up the incline. Usually he lands on his back, but he always clings to the ball. It is a marvelous performance. It always brings applause. It usually prevents a score.

On the other hand, "the other fellow" cannot play the bank, and when a Sox hit goes out there it usually leads to a score...

The playing of this left field embankment is the most spectacular and athletic fielding achievement in either league. There is nothing like it anywhere else in the country. It is easy to see how, in a close pennant race, the ability to "play the Fenway Park bank" would be the deciding factor.

Thanks to Fenway's modern amenities (for that era) and the great teams that played there — the Red Sox won the World Series that first season and three of the following six years — Boston fans quickly forgot the old dilapidated park in

was the Count Basie of PA men. ...Sherman was a character with a Capital C, and we don't have many left in this town."

Not only was Feller one of the most distinct of the "old-time" public address announcers, the Army veteran was an accomplished entertainer, a songwriter and a composer, who wrote the hit tunes, "Summertime, Summertime," "It's Easter

Time," and "She Was Five and He Was Ten."

Never one to follow a set pattern, Feller often lacked the precision of his counterparts but none could ever match his rhythm or his delivery: "Ladies and gentlemen ... Boys and girls ... Welcome to Fenway Park."

Brief at the microphone, Feller was a born storyteller away from it. As a disc jockey, Feller

interviewed the giants in entertainment from Frank Sinatra to Nat King Cole to Tommy Dorsey, and was a fast friend to all of them. Many in show biz credit Feller with hosting America's first radio talk show.

However, it was the talking Feller did from the speakers at Fenway, that brought him legendary status in Beantown.

★ FENWAY PARK ★
A TIMELINE

APRIL 20, 1912: Fenway Park officially opens.

MAY 8, 1926: The first Fenway fire occurs.

1931: The Red Sox players first wear numbers on their uniforms. The Red Sox have retired five uniform numbers: Ted Williams' No. 9, Joe Cronin's No. 4, Bobby Doerr's No. 1, Carl Yastrzemski's No. 8 and Carlton Fisk's No. 27.

JULY 3, 1932: The Red Sox play the team's first Sunday game at Fenway, a 13-2 loss to the Yankees. Sunday baseball was approved in Boston three years earlier, but not at Fenway due to its proximity to a church.

JANUARY 5, 1934: The second Fenway fire occurs.

APRIL 17, 1934: A newly rebuilt Fenway Park opens.

1936: A 23 foot tall screen is installed above the left field wall to protect the windows of buildings on Lansdowne Street, the road on the other side of the left field wall.

1940: Bullpens are constructed in front of the bleachers, replacing the old bullpen areas in the outfield foul territory beyond the dugouts.

JUNE 9, 1946: Ted Williams hits a monumental 502-foot home run to right field.

1947: Arc lights are installed at Fenway Park, making the Red Sox the third to last team among the then 16 major league clubs to do so.

OCTOBER 4, 1948: The first pennant playoff game in American League history takes place at Fenway.

OCTOBER 21, 1975: The first World Series night game occurs at Fenway Park.

1976: Fenway Park gets its first message board in center field.

OCTOBER 2, 1978: The first division-deciding playoff game in baseball history occurs at Fenway Park.

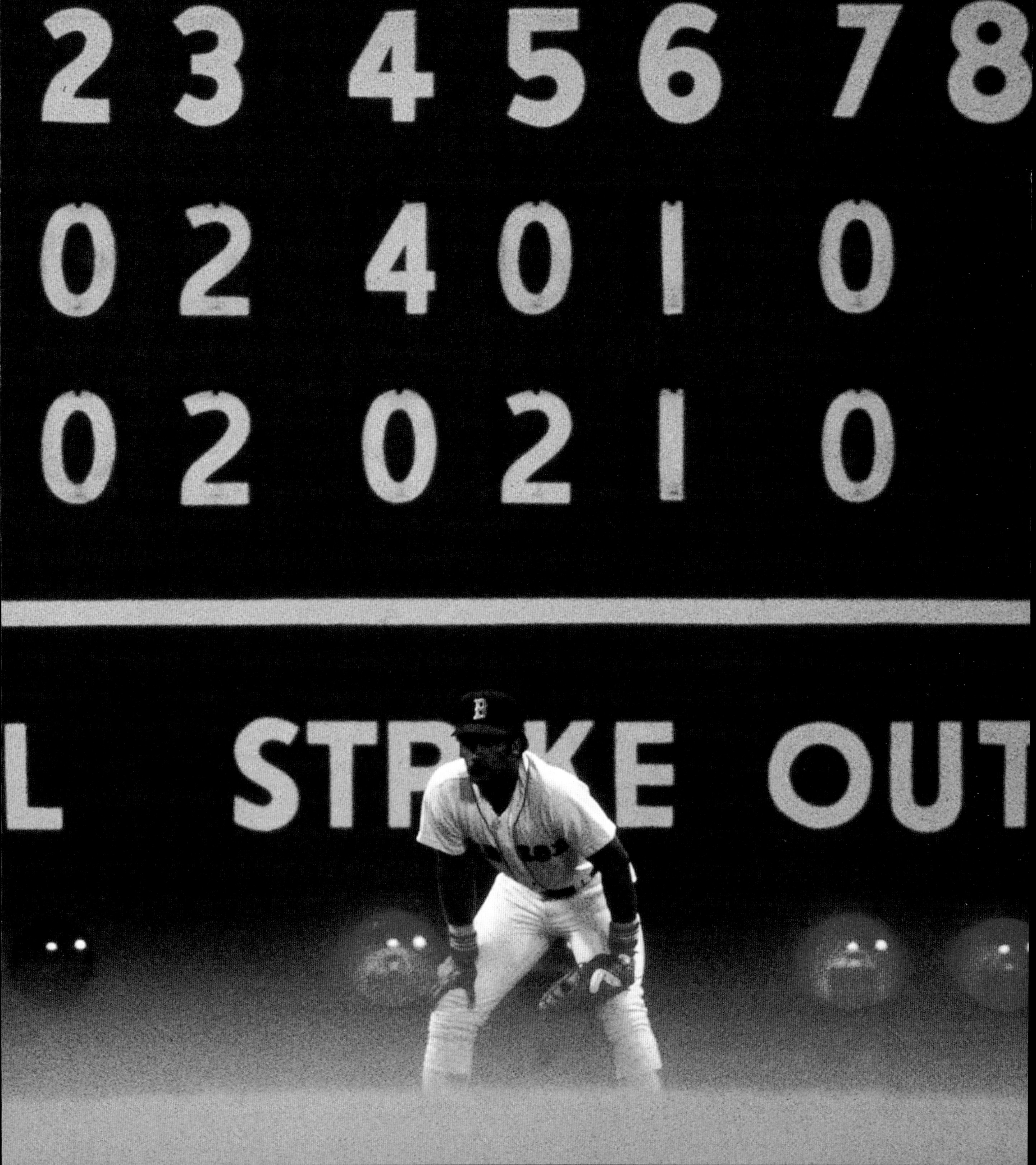
2 3 4 5 6 7 8
0 2 4 0 1 0
0 2 0 2 1 0
L STR KE OUT

which their team had played since joining the American League in 1901. The Huntington Avenue Grounds, less than a mile from Fenway Park, had spotty grass from its previous incarnation as a carnival site and a tool shed in deep center field. Nonetheless the wooden park played host to the first World Series, in 1903, when the Boston Pilgrims beat the Pittsburgh Pirates, five games to three, often with fans roped off beyond the outfield. Two Red Sox wins came via the right arm of Cy Young, whose statue now stands where the park once did, on the campus of Northeastern University.

Fenway played host to its first major league game on April 20, 1912, with Boston mayor John "Honey Fitz" Fitzgerald (the grandfather of President John Fitzgerald Kennedy) throwing out the ceremonial first pitch. News of the opening was pushed off the top of Boston's front pages by the sinking of the Titanic a few days earlier. The presence of the tall, wooden wall 315 feet down the left-field line wasn't particularly notable because that era's "dead ball" rarely traveled so far. When Hugh Bradley hit the first home run over the Wall, a local newspaper ran a cartoon with the caption, "It doesn't seem human!" While the Red Sox hit 29 home runs in 1912 (most in the American League), that total was six fewer than they had hit the previous year at the Huntington Grounds — a decline due largely to Fenway's spacious center field, where the fence was 500 feet from home plate.

"I ONLY WISH THE WALL WAS IN RIGHT FIELD."

CARL YASTRZEMSKI

OUTFIELD DIMENSIONS

Dimensions measured in feet followed by the year it changed

A
324 (1921)
320.5 (1926)
320 (1930)
318 (1931)
320 (1933)
312 (1934)
315 (1936)
310 (1995)

B
379 (1934)

C
388 (1934)

D
488 (1922)
468 (1930)
388.67 (1934)
389.67 (1954)
390 (current)

E
550 (1922)
593 (1931)
420 (1934)

F
380 (1938)
383 (1955)

G
405 (1939)
382 (1940)
381 (1942)
380 (1943)

H
313.5 (1921)
358.5 (1926)
358 (1930)
325 (1931)
358 (1933)

334 (1934)
332 (1936)
322 (1938)
332 (1939)
304 (1940)
302 (1942)

*is cited in 1931-1933 Bluebooks; this could be a misprint.

FENWAY
PARK

4 Yawkey Way, Boston, Massachusetts 02215-3496

★ **Bullpens**
The bullpens were moved from fair territory to right field in 1940 so left handers could hit more home runs.

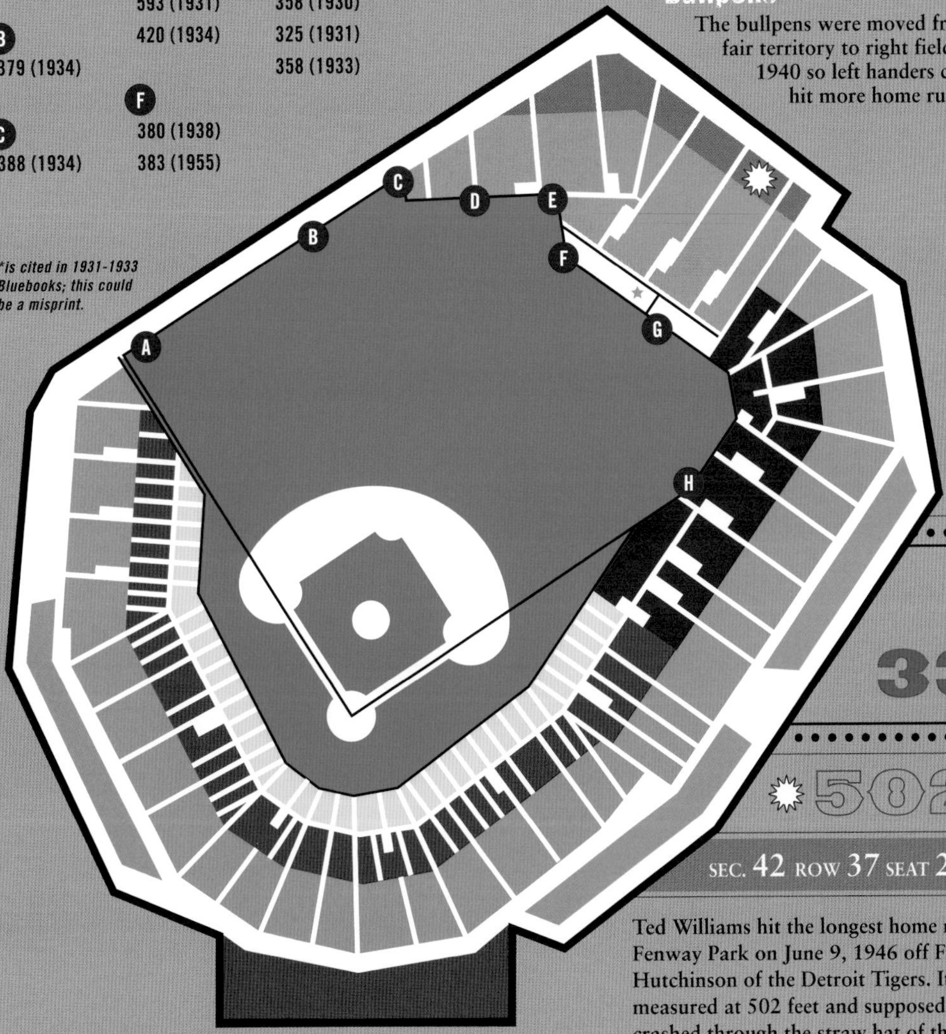

Fenway Park opened on April 20, 1912, the same day as Detroit's Tiger Stadium and before any of the other existing big league parks. It held 35,000 fans then, and today it holds 34,218. The Red Sox fit 47,627 people into Fenway for a September 22, 1935, doubleheader against the New York Yankees. Fire laws in the 1940s ended that type of overcrowding. Day game capacity has been reduced by 416 due to the glare from fan's shirts in centerfield which can affect a batter's ability to see the ball.

CURRENT CAPACITY

Day	Night
33,577	**33,993**

☀ **502'**

SEC. 42 ROW 37 SEAT 21

Ted Williams hit the longest home run at Fenway Park on June 9, 1946 off Fred Hutchinson of the Detroit Tigers. It was measured at 502 feet and supposedly crashed through the straw hat of the man sitting in the seat.

Surface:	Seating:
BLUEGRASS	**OAK**

Architect:
OSBORN ENGINEERING (1912)

Construction:
JAMES McLAUGHLIN (1912)

First Night Game:
JUNE 13, 1947

YEARS THAT FENWAY HOSTED THE ALL-STAR GAME

★ **1946** ★ **1961** ★ **1999** ★

"Any ball down the line meant the shortstop had to come out. If it hit the tin, it dropped straight down; if it hit the cement, it would bounce back hard. If it hit a bolt, anything could happen."

TED WILLIAMS

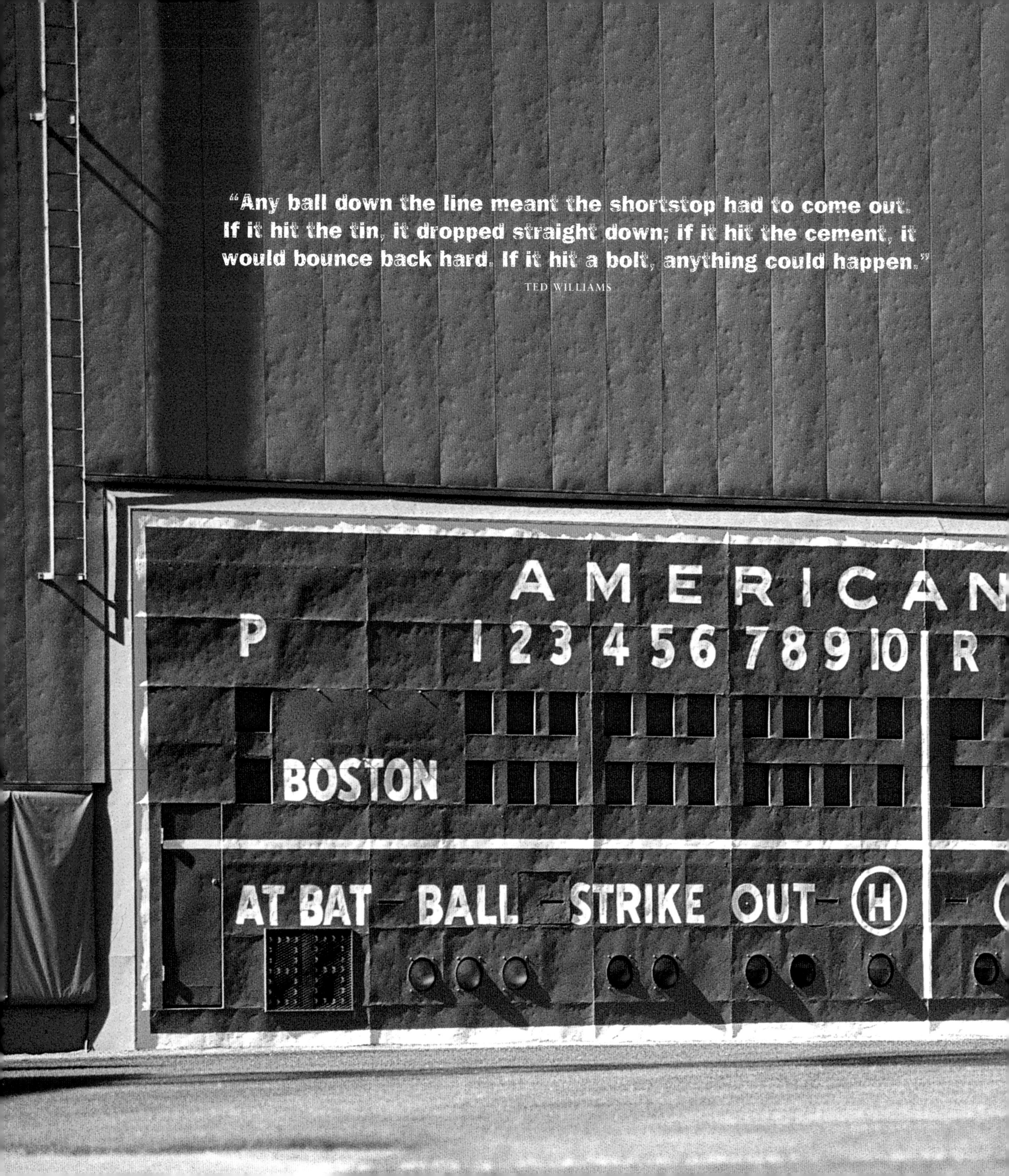

AMERICAN

P 1 2 3 4 5 6 7 8 9 10 R

BOSTON

AT BAT - BALL - STRIKE OUT - Ⓗ

JIMMY FUND

These days, with the Fleet billboard, the Coors Light billboard and, it seems, the Billboard billboard, it is tough to imagine when Fenway Park was a One Billboard, One Team ballyard.

It wasn't just any billboard; it was the Jimmy Fund sign. In Boston, a city long known for its philanthropic ways, there is no more respected and recognized charity than the Dana-Farber Cancer Institute's Jimmy Fund.

Founded in 1948, the Jimmy Fund was launched with the help of the Variety Club of New England. The club helped air a radio broadcast from the bedside of a young cancer patient — dubbed "Jimmy." The broadcast received overwhelming support from fans of the then-Boston Braves. Donations poured in and allowed for the purchase of a TV set for young "Jimmy," so the avid young fan could watch the Braves from his bed.

Five years later, under the guidance of Red Sox owners Tom and Jean Yawkey, the Jimmy Fund was adopted as the club's official charity. Over the years, the Jimmy Fund has raised more than $200 million to help aid in the treatment of what were considered incurable childhood cancers. It is now a multi-layered charitable organization with some of the country's most recognizable fund-raising events, including the Pan-Massachusetts Bicycle Challenge and the annual Scooper Bowl ice-cream bonanza.

But it is the Red Sox and the young boy "Jimmy" (the late Einar Gustafson, who died at age 65 in January 2001) for whom the Jimmy Fund always will illicit the most Boston of memories.

LEAGUE

E P   I N R P   I N R

ARTHUR D'ANGELO

He is the patriarch of the family that has sold Red Sox and baseball paraphernalia from the time of Ted to the period of Pedro. With its Yawkey Way home down the street from the Green Monster, Twins Souvenir Shop and its founder Arthur D'Angelo hardly ever have been more than a long toss away from each other.

Arthur and his late, twin brother, Henry, came to Boston from Orsogna, Italy and almost immediately started using their "twingenuity" to hawk Red Sox-related items from small sidewalk pushcarts outside the park.

Through the years, Twins Souvenir Shop (and Twins Enterprises, Inc.) has become synonymous with Red Sox gear, apparel and knick-knacks. "When we came here in

Penurious ownership led to Fenway deteriorating over the next 20 years, until the club was bought by Thomas A. Yawkey. The new owner sank $1 million Depression-era dollars into refurbishment for the 1934 season. Among many changes (like the leveling of Duffy's Cliff) was the first electric scoreboard, built into the left-field fence with red and green lights to denote balls and strikes. But what surrounded the scoreboard was a sight to behold — a 37-foot high fence extending from the foul pole to center field.

Tin advertising signs covered the fence completely, with immense messages from Calvert ("The Whiskey With the Happy Blending"), Gem Singledge Blades and Lifebuoy. In 1947, the same year lights were installed at Fenway, the signs were removed and the wall was painted a distinctive, grassy color. The Green Monster was born.

Ever since, the Wall has been like a bullfighter's cape, dangling deliciously, tempting hitters to salivate and breathe fire through their nostrils — yet often getting the last laugh. The Wall's close proximity to the batter's box wasn't nearly as ridiculous as the Philadelphia Phillies' 281-foot fence at the Baker Bowl or the New York Giants' 258-foot chip shot at the Polo Grounds, but the Green Monster's sheer size made it irresistibly tempting to batters. Righthanded hitters thrived in Fenway; Rudy York, Bobby Doerr, Jimmie Foxx and Dom DiMaggio pounded the Wall with countless line drives. Vern Stephens drove in 159 runs in

Top Red Sox hitters by position at Fenway Park

POS	NAME	AVG	GAMES	AB	H	HR
C	Carlton Fisk	.298	549	1906	568	90
1B	Jimmie Foxx	.341	438	1606	548	126
2B	Bobby Doerr	.315	954	3554	1119	145
SS	Nomar Garciaparra	.336	309	1241	417	52
3B	Wade Boggs	.370	834	3067	1134	49
OF	Ted Williams	.361	1165	3887	1403	248
OF	Tris Speaker	.353	301	1095	387	4
OF	Fred Lynn	.350	412	1482	518	69

SOURCE: PETE PALMER

1949, and the next year he and Walt Dropo each knocked in 144. Three decades later, in 1980, 5-foot-4 Freddie Patek of the California Angels hit three home runs over the Wall and a double that just missed becoming his fourth home run of the game. Though Carl Yastrzemski lamented, "I only wish the wall was in right field," lefties did benefit, too. Said Ted Williams in his autobiography, My Turn At Bat: "Even though I didn't hit out that way, I always said to myself, if you swing a little late it won't be the worst thing in the world, because there's that short fence, the defense isn't there, and slices or balls hit late can still go out. So I didn't worry about hitting late, and what did that do for me? It allowed me to develop the most valuable luxury a hitter

can have: the ability to wait on the ball."

There were drawbacks, too. Though close to home plate, the Monster's height frustrated line-drive hitters. "The Wall ruined me," Jimmie Foxx said. "I hit dozens of drives that would have been homers in any other park but they were only singles in Boston."

The Wall caused the Sox to rely too heavily on right-handed power. They traded away future Hall of Fame shortstop Pee Wee Reese because they felt he couldn't take advantage of the Wall. In 1949 the club went 61-16 at Fenway but 35-42 on the road. (Lefties rarely batted against lefties at home.) Some say the Monster chewed up and spit out George Scott, who hit 27 homers as a rookie

Top Red Sox pitchers at Fenway Park

NAME	THROWS	W	L	PCT.
Roger Clemens	R	95	55	.633
Mel Parnell	L	71	30	.703
Luis Tiant	R	69	36	.657
Joe Dobson	R	63	29	.685
Bob Stanley	R	58	43	.574
Tom Brewer	R	57	36	.613
Bruce Hurst	L	56	33	.629
Lefty Grove	L	55	17	.764

SOURCE: PETE PALMER

or crush the crowd with news of a far-off Yankees rally. Ted Williams used to talk with the scoreboard operators (usually local kids) between innings; visiting left fielder Lou Piniella would kick the wall to scare them. Their workplace is a 6- by 90-foot corridor behind the Monster, a dank and musty crawl space where they watch the action through one of six 1- by 9-inch slats. "We sit where the left fielder would be in most ballparks," said scorekeeper Rich Maloney. The corridor walls have become a three-dimensional autograph book. Dozens of players, from Jimmy Piersall to Mike Piazza, have signed their names on the concrete after venturing into the mouth of the Monster.

There are, indeed, creatures inside the Wall. One is almost solely responsible for changing the face of sports television. It was October 21, 1975, moments before Carlton Fisk's magical World Series home run. Camped out in the Green Monster to get shots looking in from left field, NBC cameraman Lou Gerard was supposed to follow any balls hit his way. But when Gerard spotted a large rat just as Fisk swung, in his moment of paralyzing panic he kept his camera on Fisk. The image that traveled through Gerard's lens and into 100 million living rooms will live forever: Fisk dropping his bat and madly motioning for the ball to land fair, bouncing on his toes while throwing his hands to the right, as if directing a jumbo jet on a runway. Seconds later Fisk leaped in glee, his home run ending what many consider the most exciting game of all time. "They didn't even know they had that shot," says John Filippelli, an associate director that night for NBC. "It was something like the sixth replay. They had no idea. It was a wonderful aberration that changed television. No one had ever thought of isolating on an individual." Ever since, directors have made sure to capture not just game action, but the emotion of the human beings who provide it.

It seems fitting that Fenway's influence will be felt forever. The Wall always has been about emotion — from frustrating pitchers to titillating hitters, from dazzling kids gazing for the first time at the old ballpark to providing old-timers the comfort that not everything has changed. The Green Monster is the largest tent stake in the world, resolutely securing baseball and Red Sox tradition as the hurricane of progress continues to blow throughout baseball. It is as textured as any flat surface ever has been.

The New Englanders

THE MEANING OF TONY CONIGLIARO

"Any Red Sox fan remembers Tony C
if they're a fan."

THE MEANING OF TONY CONIGLIARO

The letters still arrive at the Conigliaro home in Nahant. Letters, flowers, testimonials... one woman once rang the bell solemnly and donated her scrapbooks. Richie Conigliaro can go to the supermarket, to the doctor, to a beach in Aruba, and at least once a day a stranger will recognize his surname, in a flash make the connection, and the memories cascade out.

"You're Tony's brother? Oh, man, he was my idol growing up in Boston."

"Tony was so special. It was such a shame when he got beaned."

"I can still see that home run he hit at Fenway..."

"He was so dreamy. Me and my girlfriends all had crushes on him."

"What an inspiration, the comeback and all."

"He was taken so soon. The poor guy..."

The emotions range from ecstasy to agony, because Tony Conigliaro means something different to every person he touched, which was most New Englanders. There is possessiveness to people's memories: Tony C was theirs. Still is. His story has attached itself to the gene structure of every Red Sox fan, inherited by succeeding generations like DNA and dimples.

They stargazed at the hometown teenager's rise from East Boston to Fenway Park in 1964, the boys marveling at his home run power and the girls melting before his teen-idol looks. They cheered as his clutch hits and dazzling defense helped make the Sox contenders again. They wept at the news of the frightful beaning that almost killed him and knocked him out of baseball for more than a year. They struggled with him during his comeback and exulted as he returned with (what else?) a home run in his first game. They cursed his unforgivable trade to California. They celebrated his second comeback with Boston following three years in retirement. And they agonized all over again when at age 37 a heart attack left this man, once brimming with personality and promise, to spend his final eight years unable to walk or speak, taking breaths as a mere formality. To live vicariously through Tony C — which a generation of fans did — meant continual swings from hope to heartbreak, not unlike being a Red Sox fan in the first place.

Tony Conigliaro was Boston's own, enjoying a fame and following even Ted Williams never did. Carl Yastrzemski never had it, either. However talented those two were, they remained somewhat outsiders, Williams from San Diego and Yaz from Long Island. Homegrown Red Sox are embraced with consanguinity unique to New England. The rest of the country abandoned Massachusetts at one point or another; the kids from families who stayed, the ones who played stickball and halfball with six inches of snow on the ground in November, always have been put on a separate mantel. Many have felt that love over the years — from Harry Agganis to Joe Morgan to Carlton Fisk. Yet none felt it more strongly than Tony Conigliaro did. "The Chosen One," as he was dubbed early in his baseball career, became everyone's brother, everyone's son, and everyone's tragedy.

"He carried himself like he was above us. By God, then he went out and proved it. He was better than us."

Fans milling about Fenway Park on an April evening 26 years after he retired have stories at the ready. "He still carries that special image in people's hearts," says Jeff Boggier, a bank executive who was a Weymouth teenager during Tony C's heyday. "He was different. He was special. As a hometown boy he meant so much to local fans. We all followed him. It was like a cult. We don't put athletes on the same pedestal as we used to. It was more of a dreamy existence then." A fellow standing nearby adds, "Any Red Sox fan remembers Tony C — if they're a fan." Even those too young to have seen him play have been weaned on the Conigliaro legend. Says Sean Hicks, a 28-year-old Chelsean, "I hear his name everywhere. I think my mom had a thing for him. Women loved him; men wanted to be him. He was gonna be a Hall of Famer before he got beaned. I regret not having seen him play. I've seen tapes and read things, but it isn't the same." Hicks says one of his prized possessions is a Tony Conigliaro autographed baseball.

Parents named their children Tony, even Toni. Three Little League fields bear his name. Radio talk shows still crackle with listeners' memories. "Every kid my age wanted to be Tony C," one says. Recalling Conigliaro's fanciful foray into cutting teeny-bopper records in the mid-1960s, another says, "I remember this record signing Tony had at Fullerton Chevrolet in Winthrop. It was as if the Beatles were there. There were lines as far as the eye could see. Girls screaming everywhere. It was just incredible. He really was a monster on the Boston scene. We really miss him."

Like most hurricanes, he blew both in and out with startling suddenness. The Boston Record-American reported early in 1964 spring training, "Rookie May Crack Sox Outfield," and before long this teenager from Eastie would be branded on the memories of a generation. Tony C.

He hit a home run on the first pitch he saw at Fenway Park, and proceeded to slam 100 home runs faster than any American League player before or since. He dated sex siren Mamie Van Doren. He careened into bleachers after fly balls. He sang on Merv Griffin's TV show. There seem to be two kinds of athletic heroes: those who keep their head down in humility, and those who keep their head up, bursting with a fantasia of confidence and charisma. When during his first spring training Ted Williams offered him a Cadillac if he caught a tough fly ball, Tony C replied, "I already have a Cadillac." He strutted through his competition at 1964 spring training. As one teammate recalled in David Cataneo's fine biography, *Tony C*, "He carried himself like he was above us. By God, then he went out and proved it. He was better than us."

CARL YASTRZEMSKI, REGGIE SMITH, TONY CONIGLIARO

"It was as if the Beatles were there. There were lines as far as the eye could see. **Girls screaming everywhere.** **It was just incredible.** He really was a monster on the Boston scene. **We really miss him.**"

ormer Red Sox pitcher Bill Monbouquette grew up in Medford, Massachusetts, less than 10 miles north of Fenway Park. "I was a Boston Braves fan originally. Their great lefthander, Warren Spahn, was my hero. When the Braves left town after the 1952 season I became a Red Sox fan, and I loved to watch Ted Williams.

"The Red Sox gave me a tryout before a game in June 1955. My parents and I stayed to watch the game after the Red Sox signed me. A couple of toughs spilled beer on my mother, so my father and I took care of them. I was in handcuffs until the Red Sox vouched for me.

"I remember my first game was against the Detroit Tigers, and they hammered me. They scored five runs and Billy Martin stole home. The next time he came up, I unloaded on him. When he trotted by me he said, 'I guess you owed me that one, rook!'

"When I pitched for the Red Sox we only averaged 8,000 to 10,000 fans a game. *Not only could I hear every word the fans yelled, but I recognized a lot of the voices.*"

MEMBER OF THE BOSTON RED SOX

1958-1965

ILL MONBOUQUETTE

Medford, Massachusetts

CAREER STATS						
W	L	PCT	G	IP	SO	ERA
114	112	.504	343	1961	1122	3.68

To New Englanders, he was one of them. Born on January 7, 1945, Anthony Richard Conigliaro spent most of his childhood in East Boston, 15 minutes from Fenway Park, his upbringing as idyllic as it was identifiable. Strict but encouraging father Sal; loving, lasagna-at-the-ready mother Teresa; Catholic school education. "The only 'A' I ever got on my report card was A. Conigliaro," joked Tony, who preferred stealing his mother's broom handles to play stickball and halfball until his hands bled. A local legend from Little League on, Conigliaro signed with the Red Sox for a $22,000 bonus out of St. Mary's High School in Lynn. He launched his pro career by hitting .363 with 24 home runs and 74 RBIs in 83 games and winning MVP honors in the New York-Penn League. Attending spring training with major leaguers only a few months after turning 19, he doubled three times in his first start. News flowed from Scottsdale, Arizona, back to Boston that a hometown teenager could open the season with the Sox; 25 letters a day flowed back from fans to Tony C with good wishes, and one marriage proposal — from a 12-year-old girl. As camp wound down, manager Johnny Pesky had little choice but to start the slugging phenom in center field come Opening Day: "Do you want me to get shot by the fans back home?" he asked. "Yes, Tony will be in there."

Hitting a home run in his first Fenway Park at-bat launched Conigliaro into stardom. Fans mobbed his car for autographs after the game. The Sox had been a mediocre bunch in the early 1960s, but the torpor lifted thanks to a kid who still lived at home, eating his mother's breakfast of juice, cereal, bananas and strawberries every morning. By this time the Conigliaros had moved 10 miles north to Swampscott, sparking a tug-of-war between Eastie and the town that sports writers mistakenly said the new hero was from. "Swampscott Claim Resented," declared a headline in the Boston Globe. An East Boston liquor store owner, who displayed a picture of Tony C in a Red Sox uniform in his window, told the paper, "The kid is our boy. He's from up on the hill, Crestway Road. We all watched him growing up playing ball." Another Eastie native, identified as Francis (The Fastman) Valenti, said, "He's traveled most of his life on an East Boston passport. It's the fatherland."

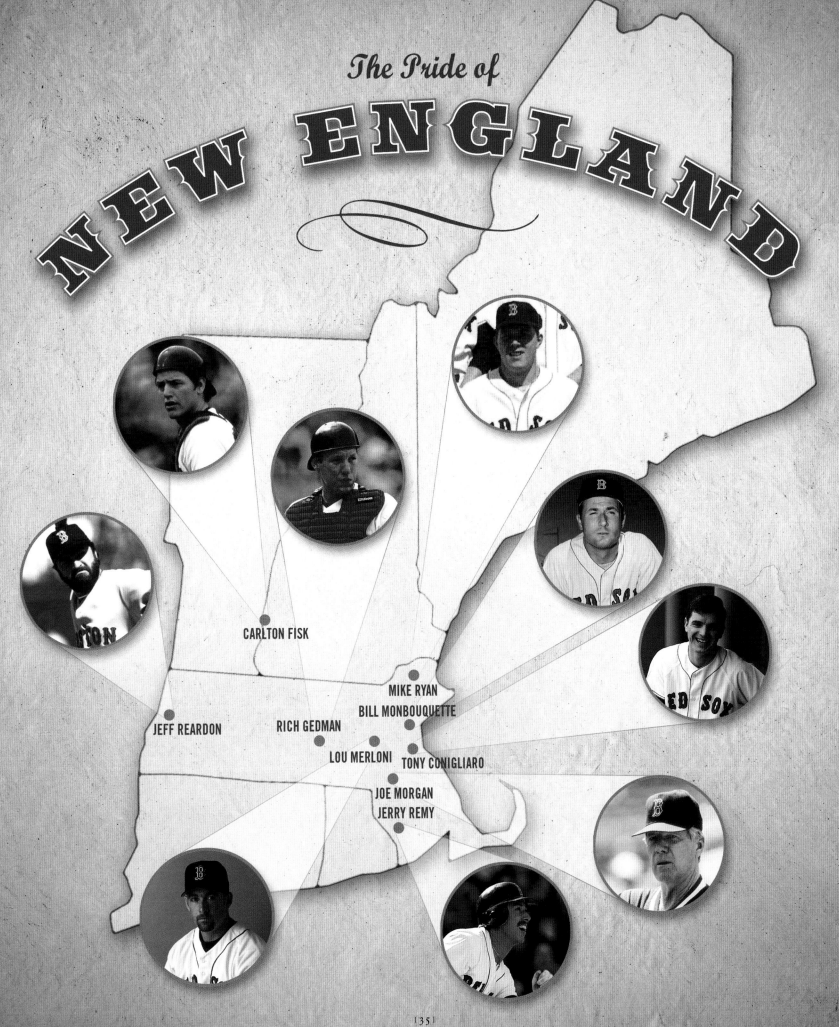

The Pride of

NEW ENGLAND

CARLTON FISK

MIKE RYAN
BILL MONBOUQUETTE

JEFF REARDON   RICH GEDMAN

LOU MERLONI   TONY CONIGLIARO

JOE MORGAN

JERRY REMY

"With all due respect to **Ted Williams,**
Conigliaro should at his present progress exceed
the great record that Williams established. Not in
batting average, but in home runs and runs
batted in and certainly in defensive play."

Conigliaro batted .290 and hit 24 home runs in 1964 at the age of 19. He would have hit more homers but for the six weeks he missed late in the season after a pitch broke his right arm. The following season, he slammed 32 homers, becoming the youngest AL player ever to win a home run title. "Some say he was the best-looking young hitter they've ever seen," said Pesky. Remembers Jim Kaat, then a young pitcher for the Minnesota Twins, "Tony C had the perfect swing for Fenway Park: Great power, lots of lift. He would have hit a lot of home runs there." The most similar ballplayers at age 20 in baseball history were Mickey Mantle and Frank Robinson, both Hall of Famers. One team's scouting report read, "With all due respect to Ted Williams, Conigliaro should at his present progress exceed the great record that Williams established. Not in batting average, but in home runs and runs batted in and certainly in defensive play."

Conigliaro played just as hard off the field. He was single, good-looking, had gaggles of girls following him, and enjoyed every minute of it. Teeny-boppers would drive to the family's home at 35 Parsons Drive and ask to see Tony; he would look out the window to see how attractive they were before deciding if he was home. He jumped on stage in nightclubs to sing, and even recorded a few singles, "Little Red Scooter" and "Playing the Field." He tantalized girls by declaring his permanent bachelorhood. Mod before anyone really knew what mod was, Tony C loved to flaunt his wares. Infielder Dick Williams was assigned to room with him on road trips in 1964 to lend a veteran influence. "The setup lasted just two months," Williams later said. "Because during that time, I never saw him. Not late at night, not first thing in the morning, never. I was providing veteran influence to a suitcase."

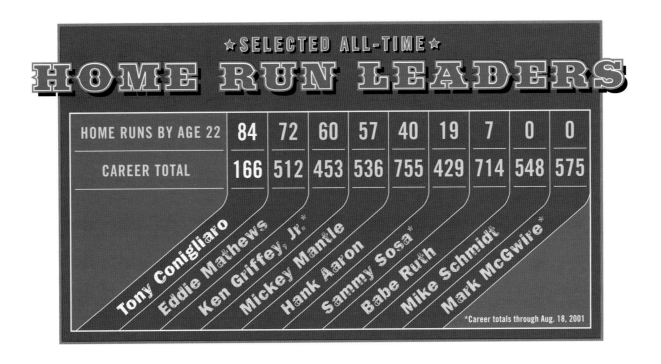

★ SELECTED ALL-TIME ★
HOME RUN LEADERS

	Tony Conigliaro	Eddie Mathews	Ken Griffey, Jr.*	Mickey Mantle	Hank Aaron	Sammy Sosa*	Babe Ruth	Mike Schmidt	Mark McGwire*
HOME RUNS BY AGE 22	84	72	60	57	40	19	7	0	0
CAREER TOTAL	166	512	453	536	755	429	714	548	575

*Career totals through Aug. 18, 2001

There was no greater sign of Conigliaro's cockiness than the way he crowded the plate. Leaning in with his bat at the ready, almost daring pitchers to throw him inside, he often would not even jump out of the way when a pitch came sailing at him — he would move only his arm, his leg, his head, to get out of the way. That is the way of a legend. Says former teammate Ken Harrelson, "Once Tony got in the box, he was there. If you threw at his ribs, that's where you hit him. If you threw at his hands, that's where you hit him. If you threw at his knee, that's where you hit him. He just did not move. He was totally fearless." Chicago White Sox manager Al Lopez is quoted in Tony C as saying, "He attacks the ball. Those are the guys who are great hitters. But I must say this: If he continues to stand as close to the plate as he does and his reflexes and reactions don't become much sharper, he's going to get hit often and will be in danger of getting seriously injured. The pitchers simply aren't going to let him keep on challenging them the way he does right now. They'll throw in on him." Red Sox coach Bobby Doerr would pitch tennis balls inside to Conigliaro so the kid could practice getting out of the way. But Tony C paid little mind. He told the Record-American in January 1966, "I'm not going to change my batting style. You just can't let the pitchers force you into that in the major leagues or you're a dead duck."

Red Sox fans know where they were when Jack Hamilton's fastball cracked into Tony Conigliaro's face like a lightening bolt. It shares the where-were-you-when-JFK-was-shot horror, resonating with the same sudden senselessness. The newspaper pictures of Tony C in the hospital, his left eye so grotesquely swollen shut and black that it looked as if it had been torn from his skull, hit fans with such force they felt like they too had been hit by Hamilton.

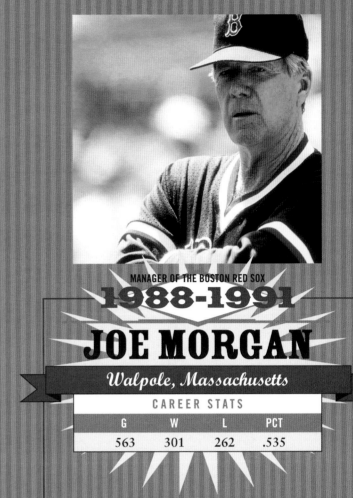

MANAGER OF THE BOSTON RED SOX

1988-1991

JOE MORGAN

Walpole, Massachusetts

CAREER STATS

G	W	L	PCT
563	301	262	.535

Former Red Sox manager Joe Morgan grew up in Walpole, Massachusetts, and has lived there all his life. He spent 40 years in professional baseball, including managing the Red Sox from the middle of the 1988 season through 1991.

"I remember we would get on a bus in Walpole Center and it would drop us off on Huntington Avenue by Wentworth Institute. Then we would walk across the Fens to the park. *The thing I will always remember is one minute you were in the middle of the city with concrete, and cars and buses, and the next minute you would come out of the tunnel and there was this beautiful ballpark.*

"We used to go to as many doubleheaders as we could; two for the price of one. We tried to get there early so we could watch batting practice. When I first watched the Red Sox they had players like Lefty Grove and Joe Cronin. My favorite was Jimmie Foxx. I used to love watching his long home runs.

"My first and only at bat in Fenway Park came in 1959 when I was playing for the Kansas City Athletics. I hit a triple off the left-center field wall. Not many guys can say they have a lifetime average of 1.000 in Fenway Park.

"I was named interim manager of the Red Sox on July 14, 1988. My first time out on the field as manager was to check on the rain. The game was called at 9:30 p.m. that night. The team went on to win 12 straight games, so I was undefeated as manager for 13 days."

1969-1980

CARLTON FISK

Charlestown, New Hampshire

CAREER STATS

G	AB	R	H	HR	RBI	AVG
2499	8756	1276	2356	376	1130	.269

Former Red Sox catcher Carlton Fisk, a member of the Baseball Hall of Fame, was born in Bellows Falls, Vermont, and grew up in Charlestown, New Hampshire.

"I was a big Red Sox fan growing up. When I first started following the team, Ted Williams was in his final years. Then I got to watch Carl Yastrzemski in his early years. It was a big thrill to play with Yaz later on.

"It was a long trip from Charlestown to Fenway Park. I'm not sure how old I was when I went to my first game, but I remember they played the Detroit Tigers.

"I can remember looking down at the field and thinking how great it would be to play there."

"What I remember best about my first game at Fenway was walking into the dugout and looking out at the left-field wall. I couldn't believe how big it was and how green it was.

"After I went to Chicago, I used to look in a mirror and see myself in a White Sox uniform and wonder what I was doing there. There was never any doubt that I would go into the Hall of Fame with a Red Sox cap. I grew up a Red Sox fan. I played for the team — not many New Hampshire boys get to do that."

The 1967 season — "The Impossible Dream" season — had been marching on with a quickening drumbeat. The American League could not wipe its feet on the Red Sox anymore. Boston, Minnesota, Detroit and Chicago were fighting for the pennant in the most entangled four-team race the major leagues had ever seen. The tension went far beyond that for the Red Sox. Dick Williams had returned as a militaristic manager, clashing openly with youngsters George Scott, Mike Ryan, Rico Petrocelli and, most of all, Conigliaro. The charismatic Tony C's style differed with Yastrzemski's all business approach. But they were yin and yang batting third and fourth. Yaz was on his way to a Triple Crown. Conigliaro made two superb catches in the All-Star Game (the first ever televised in prime time) and on July 23 the 22-year-old slugger hit the 100th home run of his career — the youngest American League player ever to reach that level.

Then came the moment that forever will sadden Red Sox fans. Batting against the Angels' Hamilton on August 18, a pitch sailed in on him with such unforgiving swiftness that Conigliaro barely could flinch in defense. He undoubtedly thought the ball would defer to him, bent by youth's magnetic field. It did not. "As soon as it crunched into me," he said later, "it felt as if the ball would go in my head and come out the other side." The pitch cracked Conigliaro's cheekbone, dislocated his jaw, severely bruised his left eye, and caused such damage inside his mouth that it filled with liquid and left him gasping for air, wondering if he would suffocate right there in the Fenway Park dirt.

"Had the pitch been two inches higher," the team physician said the next day, "Tony would have been dead." Responding to the 10,000 pieces of fan mail that flooded Sancta Maria Hospital, Conigliaro boldly declared he probably would be back in a few weeks.

Of course, he wasn't. Beyond the blurriness, a cyst on Conigliaro's retina caused a blind spot at the focal point of his already limited vision. He didn't play as the Red Sox still captured the AL pennant and played the Cardinals in the World Series, losing in seven games. It is painfully poignant for Boston fans to remember that Conigliaro's replacements, Ken Harrelson and Jose Tartabull, batted .115 combined in the World Series.

Conigliaro reported to spring training the following year, but it soon was evident that he was half-blind — he hit .125 with no home runs in the exhibition season. His frustration boiling, he tore up the clubhouse, throwing stools and flinging uniforms, as the realization of a career's transience overtook him. Conigliaro's vision was 20-300 and he risked permanent blindness if he continued to play. On April 4, 1968, the same day Martin Luther King Jr. was assassinated, Tony C retired. (Conigliaro sat out the 1968 season before returning in 1969.) Fans wrote and offered to donate one of their eyes. Their hero looked fine from the outside, still the strong, handsome young man he had been a year earlier. But from inside, his life had become a blur. So desperate to play again, Conigliaro considered becoming a left-handed batter; he even tried to become a pitcher in the 1968 fall instructional league.

★ TONY C ★
A TIMELINE

Tony Conigliaro, a Revere native, is signed by the Boston Red Sox at the age of 19.

1964

1965

1966 Tony is beaned by Angels pitcher Jack Hamilton. Hit in the left cheekbone, Conigliaro will miss the rest of 1967 and all of 1968. He was hitting .287 with 20 HRs and 67 RBI in 95 games.

1967

1968

1969 After a long recovery, Tony starts his first game for Boston. His dramatic 2-run 10th-inning HR gives the Red Sox a brief lead, and his 12th-inning run wins it.

1970

1971

1972 In a game against the Washington Senators, Tony and his brother Billy hit home runs for the Red Sox.

1973

1974 Tony is traded to the California Angels as part of a six-player swap.

1975

1976 Tony calls a 5 a.m. press conference to announce his retirement. Later tests will show that the sight in his left eye, injured in the 1967 beaning, had deteriorated.

1977

1978

1979 Tony signs a contract with Pawtucket of the International League in an attempt to make a comeback.

1980

1981

1982 Tony suffers a massive heart attack while being driven to the Boston airport by his brother Billy and lapses into a coma.

1983

1984

1985 Tony emerges from the coma, but brain damage keeps him in a horrific state of virtual catatonia for the next eight years.

1986

1987

1988 Tony dies of pneumonia and kidney failure at the age of 45.

1989

1990

MEMBER OF THE BOSTON RED SOX

1964-1970, 1975

TONY CONIGLIARO
Revere, Massachusetts

CAREER STATS						
G	AB	R	H	HR	RBI	AVG
876	3221	464	849	166	516	.264

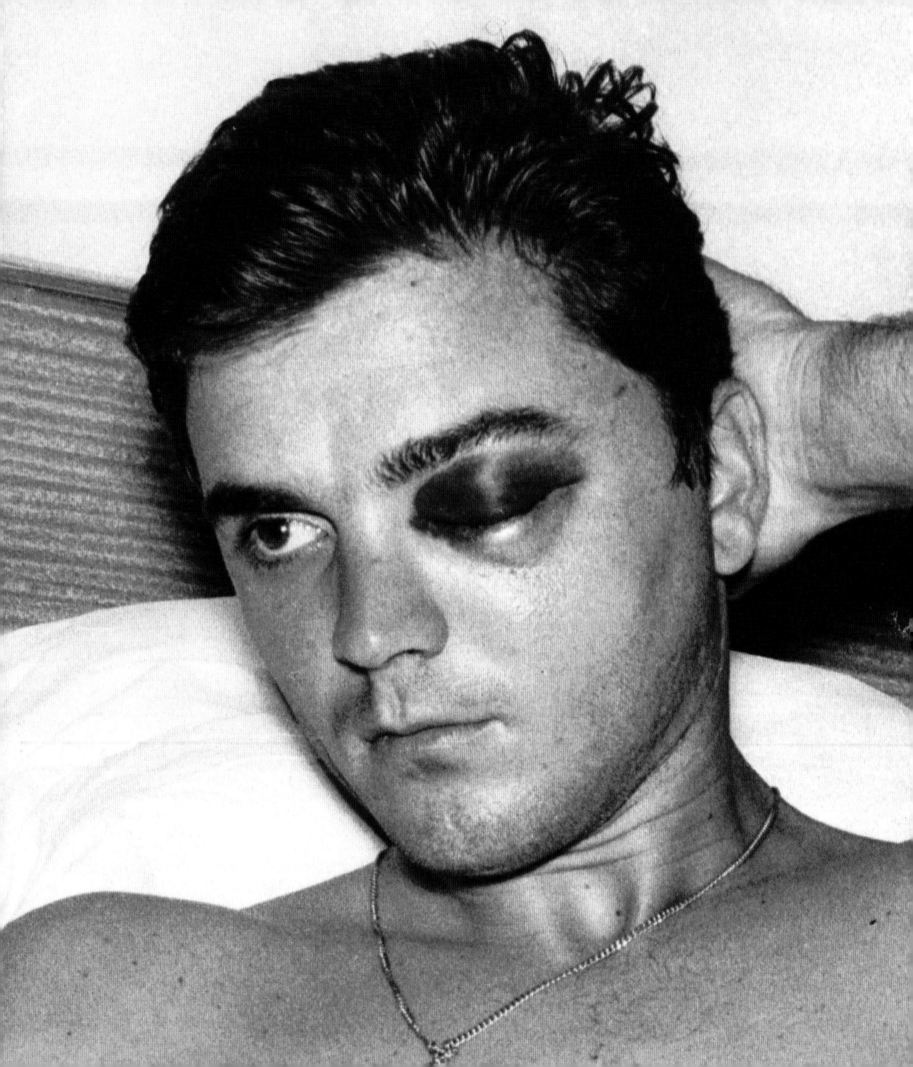

1978-1984

JERRY REMY

Somerset, Massachusetts

CAREER STATS

G	AB	R	H	HR	RBI	AVG
1154	4455	605	1226	7	329	.275

Former Red Sox second baseman Jerry Remy grew up in Somerset, Massachusetts, a small town about 50 miles south of Boston. He now is a Red Sox broadcaster.

"My grandfather and father took me to a lot of games at Fenway as a kid. I remember the long ride in on the Southeast Expressway and knowing that when I saw the light towers we were almost there. In those days not every game was televised and it was a big thrill to see a game.

The thing that impressed me most was coming up the runway into the park and seeing the field for the first time. I couldn't believe how green the field was and how high the left-field wall was. My favorite player was Yaz. If you were a young fan in 1967, he was the man. It was a tremendous thrill to become his teammate years later.

"I played very well at Fenway against the Red Sox, but it was really nerve wracking. It was the only time my family and friends got to see me play, so I was nervous, almost sick. After I was traded to the Red Sox, I became much more comfortable at Fenway. My family and friends got to see me on a regular basis so it took a lot of the pressure off. It's hard to believe, but I've now spent more time at Fenway as the TV color man than I did as a player."

By the next spring training, the clouds had begun to part. Conigliaro's vision had returned to virtually 20-20. Not quite the freakish 20-10 it had been, but good enough for him to start hitting home runs again. "Get the hell out of here!" he yelled at his first longball's persistent arc. Tony C seemed good as new — "I never saw the ball any better," he claimed — and he didn't take long to prove it. On Opening Day 1969 at Baltimore, he hit a 10th-inning home run and scored the winning run in the 12th as the Sox beat the Orioles, 5-4. "CONIGLIARO DOES IT!" the Record-American's front page screamed. A week later, in his first game back at Fenway Park, the crowd didn't wait for Conigliaro's name to be announced during pregame introductions. As soon as Sherm Feller uttered, "And No. 25..." the crowd let loose with what one newspaper called "one of the greatest ovations ever tendered an athlete." During the ninth inning, a half-dozen jubilant fans hopped over the fence to mob Conigliaro in right field and congratulate him on his comeback. "Somebody Up There Likes Tony Conigliaro," read a Record-American headline.

Tony C batted .255 with 20 home runs and 82 RBIs in 1969, perhaps the most deserving player ever to be honored with the Comeback Player of the Year award. But he was having a harder time than anyone knew. Conigliaro couldn't pick up the spin on the baseball as well as he once did, and bright sunlight (at a time when many games were during the day) caused him severe headaches. At one point he complained about the glare off fans in Fenway Park's center field bleachers; the Red Sox responded by calling that section "Conig's Corner" and implored fans to wear dark-colored clothing to help their hero. With new layers added to his story, Conigliaro's celebrity grew: He enjoyed a salacious fling with Mamie Van Doren (who had appeared in Playboy) and made guest appearances on "To Tell The Truth," "The American Sportsman" and, naturally enough, "The Dating Game." He made such an impression on screen that a Hollywood movie producer, thinking a young unknown could be just what his film needed, considered Conigliaro to fill a role for a young Italian. Instead the producer chose Al Pacino. That movie was "The Godfather."

Conigliaro enjoyed perhaps his finest season in 1970 — 36 home runs and 116 RBIs — but behind his veil of normalcy his vision was getting progressively worse. He also was entangled in a not-particularly-private feud with teammates Carl Yastrzemski and Reggie Smith. After the season, the Red Sox did the unspeakable: They traded Tony C to the California Angels. He reported resentfully to his new team for the 1971 season, his decline accelerating. Conigliaro had been wrested from his Boston hometown and from his brother Billy, who had joined him in the Red Sox outfield. His nagging injuries while with the Angels branded him as a loafer (a curious reputation for someone with his proven ability to play through pain) and he had few friends on the club. He was playing horribly, batting .222 with four home runs on July 11, when he quite literally snapped.

During a 20-inning loss to the Oakland Athletics, in which he went 0 for 8 and struck out five times, Conigliaro got into two screaming matches with umpire George Anthony, charged after Anthony with his arms flailing wildly, and tossed his helmet in the air and hit it with his bat 50 feet down the first-base line. "The man belongs in an institution," Angels manager Lefty Phillips said, dead serious. Conigliaro pretty much agreed. He called a 5 a.m. press conference to announce his retirement. "I almost lost my mind out there in the field tonight. When I came back to the room, I was twitching and my stomach was in knots. I thought, 'What am I doing here?... It's something that had to be done or I'd be in a straitjacket with the rest of the nuts. I was on the ledge tonight." Then he revealed that his vision never had recovered from the 1967 beaning. The middle of his vision was 20-300. He had to look slightly away from the baseball to get any kind of look at it. "It's like a hole that will always be missing dead center in the eye. Whenever I focus on anything, there's a total blind spot. My eyesight never came back to normal. When the pitcher holds the ball, I can't see his hand or the ball. I pick up the spin on the ball late by looking away, to the side. I don't know how I do it. I kept it away from the Red Sox... I had a lot of headaches because of the strain to see, my search for that damn baseball."

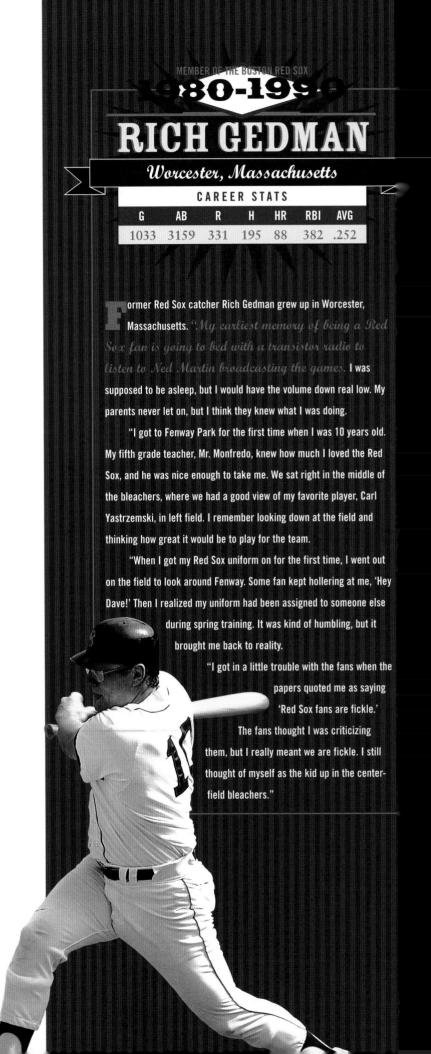

1980-1990

RICH GEDMAN

Worcester, Massachusetts

CAREER STATS

G	AB	R	H	HR	RBI	AVG
1033	3159	331	195	88	382	.252

Former Red Sox catcher Rich Gedman grew up in Worcester, Massachusetts. *"My earliest memory of being a Red Sox fan is going to bed with a transistor radio to listen to Ned Martin broadcasting the games.* I was supposed to be asleep, but I would have the volume down real low. My parents never let on, but I think they knew what I was doing.

"I got to Fenway Park for the first time when I was 10 years old. My fifth grade teacher, Mr. Monfredo, knew how much I loved the Red Sox, and he was nice enough to take me. We sat right in the middle of the bleachers, where we had a good view of my favorite player, Carl Yastrzemski, in left field. I remember looking down at the field and thinking how great it would be to play for the team.

"When I got my Red Sox uniform on for the first time, I went out on the field to look around Fenway. Some fan kept hollering at me, 'Hey Dave!' Then I realized my uniform had been assigned to someone else during spring training. It was kind of humbling, but it brought me back to reality.

"I got in a little trouble with the fans when the papers quoted me as saying 'Red Sox fans are fickle.' The fans thought I was criticizing them, but I really meant we are fickle. I still thought of myself as the kid up in the center-field bleachers."

Finally some sympathy was sent Tony C's way. Wrote Jim Murray in the Los Angeles Times, "If he took the batter's box with one leg, or one arm, or even one ear, the world would have been awed. But, to take the batter's box with one eye should be a more impressive show of courage… Tony C could fool the eye doctors and the eye charts. He couldn't fool the pitchers or the curves. The good ones had no trouble with a one-eyed man."

received a three-minute ovation. Yet his age overtook his desire. He soon had hamstring and groin injuries that kept him out of the lineup, and he lost his role to Rice, who began to blossom. Batting just .123, Conigliaro was demoted to Class AAA Pawtucket in June. He hung 'em up in August. "My only regret is that I didn't get to play as a mature athlete," he later said. "If I stayed healthy, I would have given Aaron a shot."

"As soon as it crunched into me, it felt as if the ball would go in my head and come out the other side."

TONY C

And with that, Tony C was gone. He packed up, moved back to New England and opened a golf course and restaurant in Nahant a few miles south of Swampscott. In 1975 he got the itch to play again and at the age of 30, despite having not played competitively in almost four years, beat out Jim Rice (who had won the International League triple crown the previous season) as the Red Sox's designated hitter. Yet another amazing Tony C comeback was capped on opening day, April 8, when he singled at Fenway Park in the first inning and

Conigliaro became a successful television broadcaster in San Francisco — despite a Boston accent that overwhelmed even the strictest speech classes — thanks to his charm and affability. Critics claimed he was too clunky to even correctly pronounce his own name. "Yeah, but it's a tough name," he replied. In January 1982 he auditioned as the color man for Red Sox television broadcasts and was convinced he had the job. The next day his brother Billy was driving him to the airport for a flight to San Francisco where he planned to

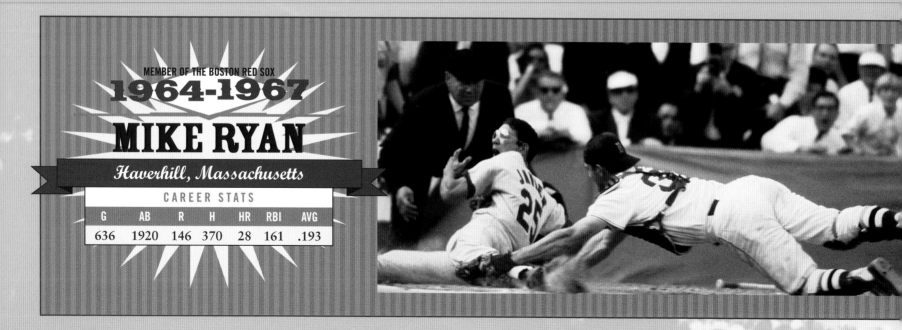

MEMBER OF THE BOSTON RED SOX

1964-1967

MIKE RYAN

Haverhill, Massachusetts

CAREER STATS

G	AB	R	H	HR	RBI	AVG
636	1920	146	370	28	161	.193

BOX SCORE
August 18, 1967

RED SOX 3, ANGELS 2

California	ab	r	h	rbi		Boston	ab	r	h	rbi
Cardenal cf	4	0	0	0		Andrews 2b	3	0	0	0
Fregosi ss	4	0	0	0		Adair 3b	3	0	1	0
Hall rf	4	2	2	2		Yastrzemski lf	3	0	0	0
Mincher 1b	4	0	1	0		Scott 1b	4	0	1	0
Reichardt lf	3	0	0	0		Smith cf	4	0	0	0
Rodgers c	2	0	0	0		Conigliaro rf	1	0	1	0
Knoop 2b	3	0	1	0		Tartabull rf	1	1	0	0
Werhas 3b	2	0	0	0		Petrocelli ss	3	2	1	1
Repoz ph	1	0	0	0		Howard c	3	0	0	0
Held 3b	0	0	0	0		Bell p	3	0	2	1
Hamilton p	1	0	0	0						
Satriano ph	1	0	0	0						
Kelso p	0	0	0	0						
Coates p	0	0	0	0						
Morton ph	1	0	0	0						
Cimino p	0	0	0	0						
Totals	30	2	4	2		**Totals**	28	3	6	2

California	ip	h	r	er	bb	k		Boston	ip	h	r	er	bb	k
Hamilton, LP	5	4	2	2	1	5		Bell, WP	9	4	2	2	1	5
Kelso	.2	1	1	1	2	0								
Coates	1.1	1	0	0	0	1								
Cimino	1	0	0	0	0	2								

California	000	000	101 – 2
Boston	000	201	00x – 3

E–Fregosi. DP–California, Boston. LOB–California 2, Boston 7. 2B–Bell.
3B–Petrocelli. HR–Hall 2(19). HBP–Conigliaro (by Hamilton)
T–2:16. A–31,207

Former Red Sox catcher Mike Ryan grew up in Haverhill, Massachusetts, just south of the New Hampshire border. His professional baseball career spanned 35 years; he was a member of the Red Sox's 1967 "Impossible Dream" team.

"As far back as I can remember, baseball was a major topic of conversation in our house. Whenever there was a family gathering, after we got caught up on the news, the conversation would turn to baseball.

"Jack Ryan, who was a cousin of my grandfather, caught for the Boston Beaneaters (later renamed the Braves) and played in the major leagues for 13 seasons. Jack was a coach for the Red Sox from 1923 to 1927. My Uncle Paul was a minor league pitcher, and my father was an outstanding athlete.

"I used to go to Fenway Park on the bus with the other kids from the local playground. We all fantasized about standing at home plate in a Red Sox uniform. We all dreamed about growing up to play for the Sox.

"The first time I played at Fenway Park I was 17 years old playing in a Hearst Corporation All-Star game. When I got to the big leagues with the Red Sox it was always a thrill to walk onto the field at Fenway. *I think every kid in New England dreams about playing for the Red Sox someday. I was fortunate enough that my dream came true.*"

MEMBER OF THE BOSTON RED SOX

1990-1992

JEFF REARDON

Dalton, Massachusetts

CAREER STATS

W	L	PCT	G	SV	IP	SO	ERA
73	77	.487	880	367	1132	877	3.16

Former Red Sox reliever Jeff Reardon grew up in Dalton, Massachusetts, in the western part of the state, and graduated from the University of Massachusetts. He was a premier closer for 14 years in the major leagues, including three with the Red Sox.

"I was a big Red Sox fan from the time I was a little kid. I used to listen to Ned Martin broadcasting the games all the time. And I used to keep score while I listened to the games.

"I remember my first trip to Fenway Park was with one of the local youth groups. Before we went to the game we all had to go to church. We trouped into a church near Fenway, and there was Carl Yastrzemski sitting a couple of rows in front of us. The counselors kept telling us we couldn't bother him but we were pretty excited.

"My favorite Red Sox player was Jim Lonborg. I was a big Red Sox fan, but I always loved to watch Tom Seaver pitching for the Mets.

"When I joined the Red Sox I had been a big leaguer for 11 years, but it was still a big thrill to play in Fenway Park. *It was pretty ironic that I always sat way out in right field or the bleachers as a kid, and then I spent my whole career with the Red Sox out in the bullpen.* It was pretty easy to look around and spot where I used to sit."

wrap up his affairs when something went terribly wrong. Tony C stopped breathing, and he clutched his chest with his fists clenched. "A tear came out of his left eye," Billy said. Billy raced 85 mph down 1-A — the same speed and the same route Tony C used to drive to play at Fenway Park — to a hospital. The heart attack cost Tony C's brain six minutes of oxygen and left him in a deep coma. This otherwise healthy man, who never smoked, barely drank and exercised regularly, was only 37. The lightening of randomness had struck him again.

He emerged from the coma four months later, but brain damage kept Conigliaro in a state of virtual catatonia for the next eight years. Drooped in bed, barely able to move or speak, he left his family and friends to wonder if he had any idea what had happened to him. They were torn between hoping he didn't and hoping he did, because if the Tony C they knew remained in that body another comeback was just a matter of time. Recalls Billy, "I just kept looking at him: 'C'mon,

Tony, one more time. You have to come around.' It was torture for us for eight years — for him not being able to come out of it, when all the other times he had.' " Stickers sprouted on car bumpers all over Boston — I PRAY FOR TONY C — and a benefit starring Frank Sinatra helped pay for his mounting medical bills. The torture crawled on, year by excruciating year. By the time Conigliaro died of pneumonia and kidney failure on February 24, 1990, it rang less of misfortune than mercy.

The legacy he left is far more complex than that of fellow teen idol James Dean or even New England's Kennedys. It goes beyond the fact that Tony C might have become one of the greatest home run hitters baseball has ever known. Former Red Sox manager Billy Herman once described Tony C's home runs as "the kind Ruth and Gehrig and Foxx used to hit." But Tony C's was an arc interrupted; he lives on as much a symbol of reverberative youth and promise as

Red Sox utility player Lou Merloni grew up in Framingham, Massachusetts, less than an hour's drive from Fenway Park. "I was about seven years old when I came to my first game. My father took me to a lot of games, and we came to the Yankees games any time we could. I got to see how the fans felt about those games. As soon as we got here, I wanted to run up the walkway to get a look at the field and see the Green Monster.

"My favorite player was Wade Boggs. I used to watch him very closely, and I was amazed at the things he could do with a bat. When his number (26) became available when I was rookie, I grabbed it. It's a big thrill to be wearing my hero's uniform number.

"My first game at Fenway happened to be the day of my parents' 33rd wedding anniversary. I had a limo pick them up to take them to the game. I had always told them that when I made it to the major leagues I would have a limousine take them to the park. My sister drove me to the game so I could ride home with my parents. She was more nervous than I was. I told her, *'All I want to do is hit a double off the wall, slide safely into second, then dust myself off, and take a minute to look around.'* My first time up, I hit a home run. About the time I was rounding second base the fans picked up the chant, 'Lou! Lou! Lou!' It's something I'll never forget."

MEMBER OF THE BOSTON RED SOX

1998-2001

LOU MERLONI

Framingham, Massachusetts

CAREER STATS*						
G	AB	R	H	HR	RBI	AVG
155	434	46	121	2	53	.279

*Through August 18, 2001

of Sisyphian persistence, of finally succumbing to one too many tragedies. His mother, Teresa, lamented, "Every time he was happiest, he got knocked down. He got beaned in Boston when he was doing so great. When he was excited he got knocked down." A Boston radio show in January 2001 paid tribute to Conigliaro; the host told the audience, "I listened to about six hours of tape the other day. I was crying, thinking of how alive he was, how vibrant he was, how much he loved playing baseball, how much he loved playing for the Red Sox." And Red Sox fans loved him for it. Still do.

"There isn't one day goes by where I don't hear something about him from somebody," says Tony C's youngest brother, Richie. "I had my finger fixed the other day. This Dr. Yee, he says, 'Conigliaro? You're not related to Tony, are ya? Oh, he was my favorite player,' this and that. Every time, everywhere I go when I say the name, it still means something. This nun from New York: 'Tony Conigliaro! I loved

Tony C!' Another time, I was in Las Vegas. I give the guy at the crap table my card. 'Conigliaro? That's not Tony, is it?' Everywhere I go. It's been so long. But people don't forget."

They don't forget the fighter who came back not once, but twice, after sitting out more than a season. They don't forget the image of his maimed eye. They don't forget him hamming it up on the "Merv Griffin Show," living life with flair and fullness and dating every pretty girl. They don't forget the home runs he launched over the Green Monster. And most of all, they don't forget that Tony Conigliaro once was just like them, growing up in East Boston, dreaming of playing ball forever. The kid practiced his stroke by swinging at a lit candle, becoming so precise he could put out the flame as the barrel whooshed by. The candle never fell over.

It still hasn't. And the way New England remembers Tony C, it probably never will.

The All-Time Starting Nine

THE GENIUS OF PEDRO MARTINEZ

As much as Fenway faithful marvel at Pedro Martinez's arm and heart, they should marvel more at his brain.

THE GENIUS OF PEDRO MARTINEZ

Press the rewind button. To find the real Pedro Martinez, you have to reverse the tape, go back in time. Fastballs zip from the catcher back to his fingers. The changeups float back. All those zeroes vanish from the scoreboards, the flag-waving crowds return home, he gets traded from the Red Sox back to the Expos and then to the Dodgers. The brawls untangle, he returns to the minors, to Triple-A, to Double-A, to Class A and beyond, all the way back to 1990 and inside the Great Falls, Montana, Dodgers team bus, traveling down one of the Pioneer League's lonely highways.

"What you got for me today?" the 150-pound pitcher says, jumping into a seat next to Guy Conti, the Great Falls Dodgers pitching coach. They have a deal: a word a day. Other players listen to stereos and play cards; most just sleep. But the hyperactive pitcher, Pedro Martinez from Manoguayabo, Dominican Republic, wants to learn a new word.

Doesn't matter what word — shoe, tractor, medicine. Conti gives Martinez the word and has him spell it, then use it in a sentence. They read signs posted on the highway and discuss what they mean. Over and over they do this as the bus rambles through Montana, Idaho, Utah. When Conti sleeps, Pedro reads newspapers, Sports Illustrated, anything. "He was clamoring to learn," Conti says. "You couldn't give him enough."

Most of the players who came to the United States from the Dodgers' academy in the Dominican would shy away from learning English, intimidated by the unfamiliar. But not this kid. Unleashed upon a world he found fascinating, not frightening, he wanted to soak it all up in a hurry. Move up. Be like Ramon, his big brother and idol, who was becoming a 20-game winner with the Los Angeles Dodgers. Be the best.

Those days were all about learning. English or baseball — give it

to Pedro, and give it to him now. He learned about mechanics. He learned about the changeup. He learned the words, then the phrases, then the idioms of English, all of it feeding his growing confidence. When the Helena Brewers manager threatened him with a beanball war, the kid looked him straight in the eye and said, "That's OK. Just remember: Your kid's throwing 84; I'm throwing 94."

That kind of velocity hardly is uncommon in baseball, but what sets apart Martinez is that his mind is just as quick. He shot up the Dodgers' minor league ladder in 1991, advancing from Class A to Double-A to Triple-A, gobbling up his lessons with striking ease and hunger. He was different. That 5-foot-10 kid, now up to 170 pounds, had a mind like a sponge and eyes like lasers.

This background information helps explain why nine years after those Great Falls bus rides, Red Sox manager Jimy Williams sits in his office after another sterling Pedro Martinez performance just shaking his head. All Williams can say to the writers is: "Do you realize what you're watching?" Whatever it is, we never have seen anything quite like it. Baseball has had its share of modern power-pitching legends, Nolan Ryan and Roger Clemens and Dwight Gooden shooting across its sky — but never one quite like Martinez, whose dominance derives as much from his brain as his body. Entering the 2001 season, Martinez was the leader among active pitchers in career ERA (2.68), opponents batting average (.206) and getting taped to a dugout pole by teammates (one). Yet he has the physical stature of a real pitcher left in the dryer too long. The naïve would mistake him for a mascot, a good-luck charm the Red Sox hang around their neck.

When Martinez stands atop the mound, baseball in hand, he doesn't just say, "You have no chance," which would suffice. He says, "I know more than you." And he proceeds to prove it. Perhaps his most defining moment came when he entered Game Five of the 1999 American League Division Series against the Indians with the score 8-8 in the fourth inning. Martinez had not started the game and was in pain because of a pulled muscle

El Tiante was known for smoking cigars. Pedro? Smoking hitters.

Martinez has developed an eerie, Buddha-like presence in baseball, a cherubic runt equal parts pitcher and poet. Paul O'Neill of the New York Yankees often doesn't even refer to him by name, instead calling him "that little Dominican fellow" — out of an abundance of respect, not a lack of it. Martinez commands the same from the press, using his precise and measured English to both inform and scold, tickle and intimidate.

The Red Sox' all-time team is a who's-who of baseball history, with names like Williams, Foxx, Yastrzemski and more. Few modern players are deemed worthy of being compared with such hallowed greats. Yet Martinez not only is the best of his era; he would have dominated against anyone. Although he missed much of the 2001 season

When Martinez studies opposing hitters, he scans for the emotional as much as the physical. "I look for everything — attitudes, frustrations, weakness," he says. "Some of them will let one at-bat frustrate them forever. All you have to do is get a pitch that's one inch away from the plate from some hitters and that will get them dragging all day and get them upset. It takes away their whole game."

behind his shoulder blade. But he spooked the Indians to the point where he gave up no hits in six shutout innings, winning the game 12-8 and the series for Boston. It was his signature performance, the one that someday could be engraved forever on his Hall of Fame plaque. "He brought normalcy to the game," Red Sox pitching coach Joe Kerrigan said afterward. "That's Pedro. That's the legend of Pedro."

That legend grows with every start, particularly at Fenway Park. Dominican fans wave flags of their home country, and their chants of "Pe-dro! Pe-dro!" echo throughout the secular cathedral. Traditional Red Sox fans join in the salute as race and class lines cross like the tangled Beantown streets outside. Boston has embraced Pedro Martinez as fondly and possessively as it has its domestic Hall of Famers, like Ted Williams, or exotic characters, like Luis Tiant.

because of a shoulder problem, his story is anything but tired. His road to Boston was as unique and stark as his repertoire. That little Dominican fellow isn't merely inside the bus anymore — he's driving it. "Once every five days," Red Sox catcher Jason Varitek once said, "New England becomes Pedro's world. The rest of us just work here."

When Martinez studies hitters, he scans for the emotional as much as the physical. "I look for everything — attitudes, frustrations, weakness," he says. "Some of them will let one at-bat frustrate them forever. All you have to do is get a pitch that's one inch away from the plate from some hitters and that will get them dragging all day and get them upset. It takes away their whole game. Sometimes I look in a batter's face for almost a minute before I pitch, just to see his attitude, his eyes, what they're gonna say."

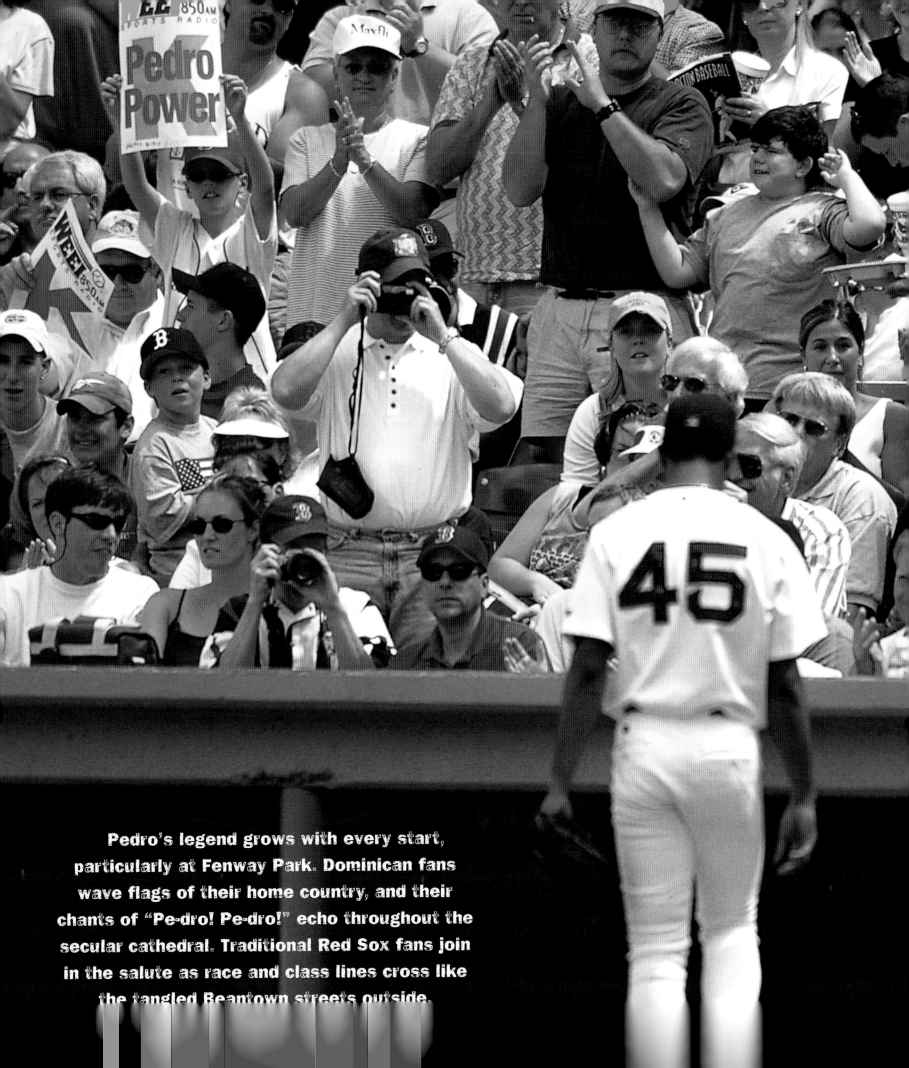

Pedro's legend grows with every start, particularly at Fenway Park. Dominican fans wave flags of their home country, and their chants of "Pe-dro! Pe-dro!" echo throughout the secular cathedral. Traditional Red Sox fans join in the salute as race and class lines cross like the tangled Beantown streets outside.

Red Sox general manager Dan Duquette, who twice has traded for Martinez, calls him the most alert and perceptive pitcher he has ever known. Like many pitchers, Martinez keeps a mental book on batters. But more than their tendencies and power zones, he senses when a hitter might be most likely to dive in to a pitch, when he isn't tracking the ball well, when he's bailing off the plate. Once an aspiring doctor — he still reads medical books from time to time — Martinez takes full X-rays of hitters when they step to the plate. Emotional MRIs.

Even baseball's top sluggers are at a loss when asked how to hit against Martinez. "For one, you go to church in the morning," Alex Rodriguez says. "He always knows what the hitter's thinking. He throws 95, 96. But if he threw 84, 85, he could still get everybody

EVEN BASEBALL'S TOP SLUGGERS ARE AT A LOSS WHEN ASKED HOW TO HIT AGAINST MARTINEZ. "FOR ONE, YOU GO TO CHURCH IN THE MORNING," ALEX RODRIGUEZ SAYS. "HE ALWAYS KNOWS WHAT THE HITTER'S THINKING. HE THROWS 95, 96. BUT IF HE THREW 84, 85, HE COULD STILL GET EVERYBODY OUT. HE'S THAT SMART."

out. He's that smart." Before his magical 1999 postseason heroics against the Indians, Martinez sat down in the dugout next to Boston's starter that day, Bret Saberhagen, and said, "These guys are gonna swing tonight. You don't have to throw them strikes." Saberhagen later acknowledged he failed to do that, got shelled, and needed Martinez to bail out the Red Sox, to show them the way. Williams almost never removed Martinez in the middle of an inning. The manager trusted Pedro to extricate himself from whatever trouble he encountered, using memory to recall the past and intellect to foresee the future. This process is overshadowed when Martinez unleashes one of his five darting fastballs, a wicked curve or a changeup with more movement than a belly dancer. It's easier to see in Atlanta Braves pitcher Greg Maddux, for example, whose mortal repertoire brings his brain to the fore. But even Maddux appreciates Martinez's control tower more than his rockets. "He's capable of blowing a lot of hitters away, but he tricks them," Maddux says. "I like the embarrassment he puts on hitters, the way he abuses them and makes them look like they don't belong on the same field with him. There's a lot of pitchers with stuff as good as his. But he says, 'Even though I'm a power pitcher, I can still pitch like I'm not.'"

Hitters like to say that the game is 90 percent mental — until they are overmatched. Then the pitcher simply has "filthy" stuff. "The bottom line is he throws three pitches and can throw them at any time in the count," says Derek Jeter of the Yankees. There is something else at work, too — an aura that erodes a batter's confidence when Pedro stares at him. Says Braves pitcher Tom Glavine, "He's elevated himself to another

"Don't mess with the master." He delivered that message through his last pitch before being hoisted atop his teammates' shoulders.

"There was a certain aura to that game when Pedro came in," Duquette says. "There was a certain respect from Cleveland fans and players for this pitcher. When they saw he was throwing like Pedro Martinez, it got quiet. It got very quiet. I knew then we were going to win the game. Pedro Martinez is what made us better than the Cleveland Indians."

Without his best stuff that night or in his next start against the Yankees, Martinez had to rely on spotting his pitches, on changing speeds. Pitching sequences and patterns. This is a man who, when he demonstrates three different grips of a changeup, moving fingers across and with the seams, looks like a pianist

"HE'S CAPABLE OF BLOWING A LOT OF HITTERS AWAY, BUT HE TRICKS THEM."
GREG MADDUX

category. That gives him a mystique about him. They're almost beat before the game even starts, they're so psyched out."

After Martinez dominated the Yankees 13-1 in Game Three of the 1999 American League Championship Series, the series effectively had been shortened to six games. All of baseball spoke of how the Yankees, their lead cut to two games to one, had better close out the Red Sox before a seventh game, when Martinez surely would smother them as he had everyone else — particularly the Indians in his Game Five relief gem in the previous round. During that game with the Indians, Cleveland catcher Sandy Alomar tried a little gamesmanship by retying his shoes after reaching first base in an attempt to slow down Martinez. The pitcher merely smirked at Alomar, as if to say,

forming a chord. His art emerged those nights against the Indians and the Yankees, leaving Yankees manager Joe Torre to say, "He's got a baseball instead of a paintbrush."

Listening to Martinez speak rivals watching him pitch. To him, games aren't "big," they "have meaning." Dominicans are his "fellows." When Red Sox shortstop Nomar Garciaparra had a big game against the Indians a few years ago, teammate Trot Nixon gushed, "Nomar's awesome, he's just a flat-out stud." Martinez described Nomar as "rich in talent," a phrase Boston writers still speak of reverently.

Martinez makes eye contact during interviews — a welcome change from many major leaguers, most of whom adopt an airy gaze, as if playing dead before a bear — and will explain himself calmly, repeatedly, if not understood. Says Tony Massarotti, who covers the Red Sox for the Boston Herald, "You feel like you're talking to a diplomat."

Dissatisfied with knowing all the current baseball idioms, Martinez has become the new Dennis Eckersley, coining his own vernacular."I don't know what the hell he's talking about most of the time," says Red Sox reliever Rod Beck. On days he is not pitching, the hyperactive Martinez will pass time chirping these phrases from the dugout. In 1999, the chatter so vexed the White Sox that they called the Red Sox's dugout and told them to shut him up. Garciaparra and pitcher Mark Portugal proceeded to tape Martinez's

made the Yankees look like the Gas House Gorillas: One, two, three strikes, you're out ... one, two, three strikes, you're out ... The following season, he out-dueled former Red Sox ace Roger Clemens in beating the Yankees 2-0 on national television. Martinez has shed the head-hunting label he gained in the mid-1990s while pitching for the Montreal Expos, when he had little control of his pitches. But he doesn't mince words when discussing his art of intimidation, which has helped make the 5-foot-11, 175-pound wisp the biggest bully in the big leagues. "You don't intimidate the guy — the ball does," Martinez says. "A man is just a man. Not because you're 6'7" and I'm 5'11" are you gonna intimidate me. If I reach back and throw a ball at your head, 98 mph, there's a big chance that if the ball hits

mouth closed, and then for good measure tie him to a dugout support pole. This topped the previous best dugout stories about Martinez, which included him wearing a Yoda mask during a game and, another time, parading around in the uniform pants of puffy reliever Rich Garces, who could audition as the Michelin man.

On days that Martinez pitches, though, his brain turns on, his eyes lock in, and nothing else exists. "A bomb could go off next to him and he wouldn't notice," Kerrigan says. Martinez recognizes when the spotlight is on him, and thrives on it. He has a 1.13 career ERA in postseason games, and often comes through with his best performances against the best teams. No onlooker will forget his 17-strikeout one-hitter at Yankee Stadium in September 1999, when he

you in the head, you're gonna get something broken, and really bad. ... Sometimes, letting them know that you're crazy enough to do anything with that ball in your hands, it's good enough to give them an impression."

Indeed, the diplomat is not always diplomatic. When asked about the Curse of the Bambino after shutting out the Yankees at Fenway Park in May 2001, Martinez snapped, "Maybe they should wake up the Bambino and have him face me and maybe I'll drill him." No doubt. When Matt Lawton of the Minnesota Twins stepped out of the batter's box just as Martinez was about to pitch in 1999, Martinez hit him in the right knee. After Athletics third baseman Olmado Saenz made no effort to get out of the way of a Martinez pitch, Martinez buried a fastball in Saenz's back, as if to say, "You want to get hit? Try this on for size."

"If you get fresh with me on the mound or do something to show me up," Martinez said after hitting Saenz, "I'll drill you."

Paulino and Leopoldina Martinez always made sure their four sons — Ramon, Nelson, Pedro and Jesus — had the proper uniform for Liceo Secondario las Americas, the high school in Manoguayabo. Khaki pants and a blue shirt. Paulino worked as an administrator at the school. Leopoldina washed the uniforms every day to make sure they looked proper.

Pedro got his best grades in English. "Lowest grade I ever had was a 98," he crows. "I was straight aces." An aspiring physician,

break his mother's heart.

"I'm almost falling asleep on the bus. I'm trying to read the books," Pedro recalls. "So maybe I should concentrate on one. And I didn't want to quit baseball because baseball was No. 1. I decided baseball didn't go along with medicine. I told my mom and she started crying. I was too good in school to just quit it like that."

Pedro's brain didn't lie fallow at the Dodgers' academy. He soaked up all he could — particularly during the morning and evening English classes that were required of all players. Pablo Peguero, the scout who signed Martinez, remembers, "The only complaint we had from teachers was that Pedro talked too much. He asked a lot of questions. He wanted to learn fast."

Pedro wanted to play baseball, too, particularly after big brother Ramon started succeeding with the Dodgers. His parents kept the hyper kid as focused as they could. "Education was very important," says Ramon, who retired from baseball in 2001. "We all went to school. Sometimes we didn't want to, but we had to. It was very important. They were like, 'You can play, but you have to go to school.'"

The same deal remained after Pedro signed with the Dodgers as a 16-year-old and entered their baseball academy in Guerra, a 45-minute bus ride from home. He had to finish high school at night. But he spent every free moment playing baseball, coming home with his school uniform dusty from the sandlots. He reluctantly decided to

Adds Arizona Diamondbacks scout Mel Didier, then a special-assignment scout with the Dodgers, "He was a guy, from the first day he was with the Dodgers, who picked up all the defenses, backups, cutoffs, relays. He did it in three weeks. Some guys spend three years and never do."

Martinez spent two years studying in Guerra before graduating to the United States in 1990, determined to move up quickly. Forbidden to run so that he could gain weight, he bribed a ballpark guard with $20 bills to let him run at night. Guy Conti, his bus-ride English teacher in Great Falls, once gave in and let Martinez run a two-mile race against 20 other pitchers; Martinez won, and afterward was seen puking out his guts.

[PEDRO MARTINEZ]
LEADS ACTIVE PITCHERS IN THE FOLLOWING CATEGORIES
[THROUGH 2000 SEASON]

WINNING PERCENTAGE
.691

QUALITY STARTS PERCENTAGE
.706

Ks/WALKS RATIO
4.11 TO 1

HITS PER 9 INNINGS
6.73

BASERUNNERS PER 9 INNINGS
9.64

OPPONENTS BATTING AVERAGE
.206

OPPONENTS ON-BASE AVERAGE
.270

OPPONENTS SLUGGING AVERAGE
.319

"... SOMETIMES, LETTING THEM KNOW THAT YOU'RE CRAZY ENOUGH TO DO ANYTHING WITH THAT BALL IN YOUR HANDS, IT'S GOOD ENOUGH TO GIVE THEM AN IMPRESSION."

PEDRO ON THE ALL-TIME LISTS

Ks PER 9 INNINGS		OPPONENTS BATTING AVG		HITS PER 9 INNINGS		Ks/WALKS RATIO		WINNING PERCENTAGE	
Randy Johnson	10.95	Nolan Ryan	.204	Nolan Ryan	6.56	**Pedro Martinez 4.11 to 1**		**Pedro Martinez**	.691
Pedro Martinez	**10.38**	Sandy Koufax	.205	**Pedro Martinez**	**6.73**	Shane Reynolds 3.92 to 1		Whitey Ford	.690
Nolan Ryan	9.55	**Pedro Martinez**	**.206**	Sandy Koufax	6.79	Doug Jones 3.68 to 1		Lefty Grove	.680
Sandy Koufax	9.28	Sid Fernandez	.209	Sid Fernandez	6.85	Bret Saberhagen 3.62 to 1		Vic Raschi	.667
Sam McDowell	8.86			J.R. Richard	6.88	Curt Schilling 3.48 to 1		Christy Mathewson	.665

[THROUGH 2000 SEASON]

PEDRO WITH FELIPE ALOU

In 1991, after little more than a year in the United States, Martinez had risen to Triple-A Albuquerque. During a road trip to Las Vegas, longtime baseball executive Syd Thrift, then a consultant to the Dodgers, was in his hotel room when Martinez knocked on the door. "I want to be the best," Martinez told Thrift, and the two talked for more than an hour about focus and concentration. Thrift filed the following report to general manager Fred Claire: "Great aptitude. Came to meet me voluntarily. Wanted to learn more about how to be successful. Could be a great one!"

The Dodgers used Martinez as a middle reliever in 1992 and 1993 before trading him to the Expos because they believed his body wouldn't withstand the rigors of pitching. Though broken-hearted to leave Ramon, Martinez found an equally important influence in Montreal: manager Felipe Alou, an erudite fellow Dominican known for his equanimity and poise. "You can't overestimate the influence that Felipe had on Pedro," says Kerrigan, the Expos' pitching coach from 1992 to 1996. "He was like his parish priest. He was like his father. Whenever Pedro strayed a little bit or drifted a little bit, Felipe would bring him back in. The long talks that they had during Pedro's maturing years have paid off now. You're seeing the result of that." Adds Martinez, "I would say 70 percent of my career has to do with the mental approach that Felipe taught me. He taught me everything I know about approaching the game and taking it serious — especially on the day I was starting. Felipe always told me: On that day you are somebody special. That's your day."

Martinez made Montreal his city. He became a crowd favorite because he was so small, so feisty (he precipitated several brawls) and so dominant (he pitched nine perfect innings in 1995 before losing the gem in the 10th). Martinez returned the affection by learning French through television and the local newspapers, and by speaking with locals around town. During his Cy Young Award season of 1997, when he was honored at a downtown restaurant for being named National League pitcher of the month for July, he delivered his acceptance speech in French, and received a standing ovation.

Ballparks around the American League tremble with chants of "Pe-dro! Pe-dro!" now. Martinez's pitches and persona captivate anyone who watches; he's not a favorite just in Boston. His magnetism is unmatched in modern baseball. Ken Griffey Jr. is old news. A-Rod makes more news with his pocketbook than his power. Mark McGwire and Sammy Sosa might paint a forceful stroke or two in an eruption of muscular might. But only from Martinez can you get two hours of adrenaline, finesse and art on a regular basis.

He understands his stature, having earned it, and bristles at any suggestion to the contrary. Martinez caused a stir two years ago by speaking out when Williams scratched him from his scheduled start because he arrived late to Fenway Park. "He didn't have any reason to embarrass me out there. If I'm a bad influence on the team, they'd better get me out of here," Martinez said. Yet his self-regard has strict limits. Any hint that he has eclipsed his big brother as a pitcher is met with a stern and stock reply. "A student," he warns, "can't ever be smarter than his teacher."

It was with this reverence that Martinez had one of the thrills of his life at the 1999 All-Star Game at Fenway Park — and it had nothing to do with him striking out the first five batters he faced as the American League's starting pitcher. Hours later, well past midnight, he went to the ballpark suite of Red Sox owner John Harrington and met Ted Williams. Martinez peppered Williams with questions about hitters, deliveries, the effectiveness of curveballs versus changeups ... for an hour and a half, leaving all who saw it with their mouths agape. Williams autographed a program for Martinez — and when the pitcher left the room, he clutched that program in his two hands, not the All-Star Game MVP trophy.

Martinez said thank you to all of his teachers — from his parents to Ramon to Conti to Thrift to Alou to Williams and more — when he spoke one morning to a Boston-area elementary school assembly. From the podium he looked out upon the sea of white tops with navy blue pants and skirts, flashed back to his youth, and smiled. "You look great in those uniforms," he told the kids. The best pitcher in the world nodded to the children's cheers, naked for everyone to see.

BASEBALL HAS HAD ITS SHARE OF MODERN POWER-PITCHING LEGENDS, NOLAN RYAN AND ROGER CLEMENS AND DWIGHT GOODEN SHOOTING ACROSS ITS SKY — BUT NEVER ONE QUITE LIKE THIS, WHOSE DOMINANCE DERIVES AS MUCH FROM HIS BRAIN AS HIS BODY.

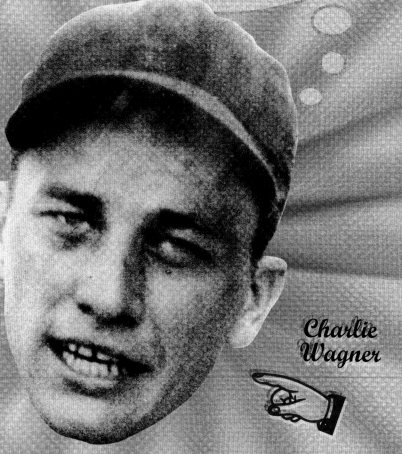

JOHNNY PESKY & CHARLIE WAGNER

PICK BOSTON'S ALL-TIME STARTING NINE

ALL-TIME BATTING ORDER

by JOHNNY PESKY	by CHARLIE WAGNER
Dom DiMaggio (or Fred Lynn), CF	Dom DiMaggio, CF
Nomar Garciaparra, SS	Bobby Doerr, 2B
Ted Williams, LF	Ted Williams, LF
Jimmie Foxx, 1B	Jimmie Foxx, 1B
Bobby Doerr, 2B	Nomar Garciaparra, SS
Carlton Fisk, C	Carlton Fisk, C
Dwight Evans, RF	Dwight Evans, RF
Frank Malzone (or Wade Boggs), 3B	Frank Malzone, 3B
Pedro Martinez, RHP	Lefty Grove, LHP
Mel Parnell, LHP	Pedro Martinez, RHP
Dick Radatz, Reliever	Dick Radatz, Reliever

 When Johnny Pesky signed with the Red Sox out of high school in 1940, little did he know that he had found a virtual lifetime employer. Except for brief detours through the Detroit and Washington organizations in the 1950s, Pesky has been drawing a paycheck from the Red Sox regularly for more than six decades. As the 21st century dawned, he was an octogenarian instructor in the organization.

Pesky, a shortstop and third baseman, played brilliantly for the Red Sox for eight years. He led the American League in hits in each of his first three seasons and ended his major league career as a .307 hitter. Pesky managed the Red Sox in 1963 and 1964, was a Red Sox coach for a decade, and has held positions in the team's minor-league and scouting departments.

Having witnessed more than 56 years of Red Sox baseball, Pesky doesn't need to research an all-time Red Sox team; he ate, slept and drank with most of the Red Sox greats.

 Nobody — not even Johnny Pesky — has been around the Red Sox longer than Charlie Wagner, who signed with the club in 1935 and entered the 2001 season as the only 88-year-old instructor/scout in the organization. Wagner's longevity earned him the honor of throwing out the ceremonial first pitch at a May 2001 game commemorating the 100th anniversary of the franchise. "It was a nice feeling to be there with all those guys," he says. "I cried through half of it. I now cry at the weather report, too."

Wagner had a modest major league career. He pitched in six seasons for the Red Sox, going 32-23 in the 1930s and 1940s. Perhaps Wagner's great claim to fame was being Ted Williams' road roommate — "Ted was a good roomy; early to bed, early to rise, and he talked baseball morning to night." Wagner left the Red Sox's active roster after the 1946 season and became a lifer in the team's minor-league and scouting departments. Like Pesky, Wagner can draw on a lifetime of memories to select an all-time Red Sox team.

JIMMIE FOXX

JOHNNY PESKY I have to pick Jimmie Foxx. I played only two months with Foxx when I got here in 1942. He was losing his eyesight, but everyone knew what he could do. Ted Williams used to talk about some of Jimmie's long home runs. My rookie year we'd go into Detroit, Chicago, St. Louis, Washington or New York, and Ted would say, "Foxx hit one there, and he also hit one there," pointing out the farthest reaches of the stands. Ted said of his era, of his time, Foxx hit balls as far as anyone did. He hit one in the third deck in Yankee Stadium. I think he's only one of five players to slug over .600 lifetime (.609). Foxx was built like a tank. He was a wonderful man, smoked a cigar, and had a great way about him. Mo Vaughn could hit too. George Scott was good, but not as good overall as Vaughn. Vaughn was Boston.

CHARLIE WAGNER Foxx is my pick, too. He could hit, run, he had one of the greatest arms in baseball, and he was a delightful man. You want distance home runs? He hit one out in New York off Lefty Gomez; it landed in the third deck. Years later Gomez said, "You know that unidentified white object we discovered on the moon? It was that homer Foxx hit off me." I had dinner with Foxx any number of times. He could drink, but nothing to excess. Every day he was on that ballfield and ready to go.

JIMMIE FOXX

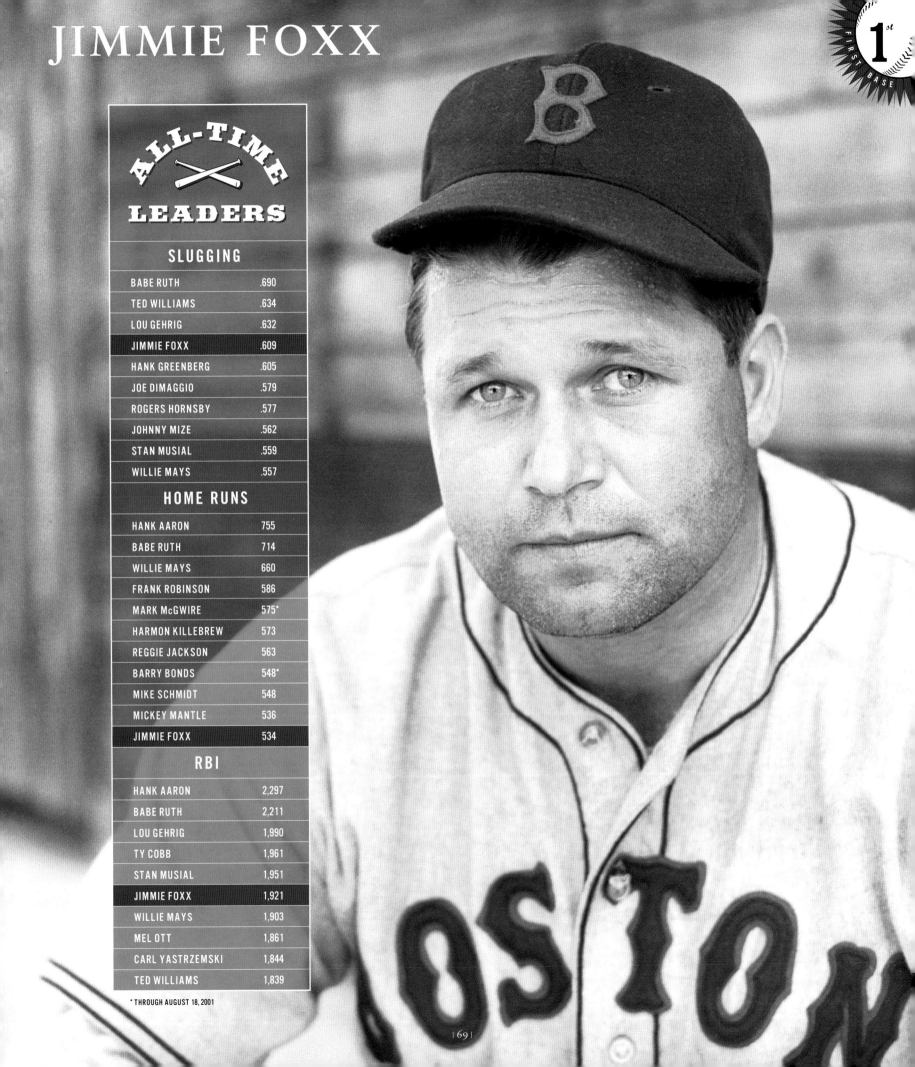

ALL-TIME LEADERS

SLUGGING

BABE RUTH	.690
TED WILLIAMS	.634
LOU GEHRIG	.632
JIMMIE FOXX	.609
HANK GREENBERG	.605
JOE DIMAGGIO	.579
ROGERS HORNSBY	.577
JOHNNY MIZE	.562
STAN MUSIAL	.559
WILLIE MAYS	.557

HOME RUNS

HANK AARON	755
BABE RUTH	714
WILLIE MAYS	660
FRANK ROBINSON	586
MARK McGWIRE	575*
HARMON KILLEBREW	573
REGGIE JACKSON	563
BARRY BONDS	548*
MIKE SCHMIDT	548
MICKEY MANTLE	536
JIMMIE FOXX	534

RBI

HANK AARON	2,297
BABE RUTH	2,211
LOU GEHRIG	1,990
TY COBB	1,961
STAN MUSIAL	1,951
JIMMIE FOXX	1,921
WILLIE MAYS	1,903
MEL OTT	1,861
CARL YASTRZEMSKI	1,844
TED WILLIAMS	1,839

* THROUGH AUGUST 18, 2001

BOBBY DOERR

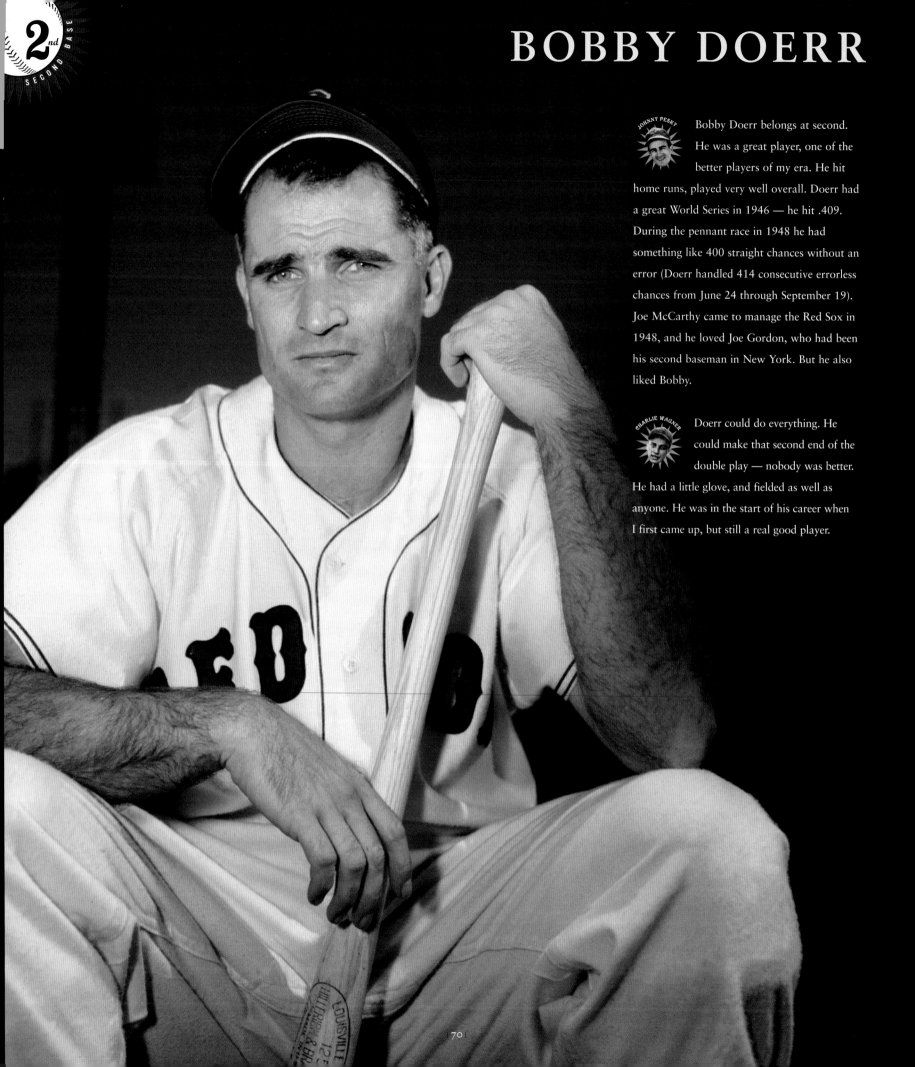

Bobby Doerr belongs at second. He was a great player, one of the better players of my era. He hit home runs, played very well overall. Doerr had a great World Series in 1946 — he hit .409. During the pennant race in 1948 he had something like 400 straight chances without an error (Doerr handled 414 consecutive errorless chances from June 24 through September 19). Joe McCarthy came to manage the Red Sox in 1948, and he loved Joe Gordon, who had been his second baseman in New York. But he also liked Bobby.

Doerr could do everything. He could make that second end of the double play — nobody was better. He had a little glove, and fielded as well as anyone. He was in the start of his career when I first came up, but still a real good player.

JOHNNY PESKY I take Nomar Garciaparra, though I liked Rico Petrocelli because he hit a lot of home runs. I think Petrocelli was the first American League shortstop to hit 40 homers in a year — and he was a good all-around player. I liked Rick Burleson and Luis Aparicio, too. But Garciaparra can do it all: steal a base, hit a homer, play the field, and he's led the league in hitting. On fielding alone, I would pick Aparicio. Joe Cronin was a great hitter, but he was winding down his career when I came up. He was a player-manager and usually just pinch-hit. Then he turned the managing over to me.

CHARLIE WAGNER Cronin and Garciaparra. Cronin was a tough two-strike hitter. Didn't bother him one damn bit to hit with two strikes on him. Garciaparra is everything you want in an offensive player, and he's as good at defense as there has ever been. He has a great arm.

SHORT STOP SS

WADE BOGGS

I see only two people: Wade Boggs and Frank Malzone. Boggs has a chance to go into the Hall of Fame. He had 200 hits and 100 walks in the same season four times. Only Lou Gehrig did it more — seven times. Boggs was what you call a pure hitter. He could handle the bat as well as anyone who's ever played the game. He was like a great violinist, a virtuoso with a bat in his hands. He kept in shape and he spent a lot of time practicing — I always admired him because he worked so hard. I hit him grounders every day, and he worked at becoming a good fielder. Malzone was a great fielder, had power, and played hard.

I take Malzone. He was one of the great fielders. He was a great help to Boggs when Boggs first came up — he helped him to no end on learning how to play third base. The hitting part, Boggs didn't need any help. For his type hitter, there was nobody to match him. And he could have been a home run hitter if he wanted to. Except for Ted Williams, I can't recall anybody who could put the bat on the ball as often as Boggs did and hit it as solidly. Boggs was hitting .300 every year in the minor leagues. The reason they kept him in the minor leagues for four or five years is that he couldn't catch a ball.

FRANK MALZONE

Carlton Fisk is the best catcher we ever had. He worked hard at it, and he deserved everything he got. He'd go through all those mannerisms at the plate — you'd think he was in pain and coming apart at the seams. But he was gamer, and he'd come through for you in the clutch.

Fisk is my choice, too, and I have another guy named Moe Berg. Fisk came fast. I had him as a kid when he first came to spring training with the big club. He didn't have a glove, and as he walked by I said, "Hey young man, where's your glove? What position do you play?" He said, "I play catcher. I thought they gave you gloves here." The Rawlings glove people were there, and I said, "You'd better go get yourself a glove" — and that's probably the best advice I ever had for him. The pitchers liked to throw to him because he didn't miss any balls. He didn't do anything stupid. He just had a real presence on the field.

Berg couldn't hit too well, but he was a pitcher's catcher. They're always asking if a catcher can hit — that isn't always the thing. The game starts when the pitcher throws the ball. And that's where a good catcher makes the whole story. A pitcher has a good feeling about a catcher that looks as big as the building he's in. Berg was one of those guys.

TED WILLIAMS

 I'd have to pick a couple of guys at each position. Ted Williams, of course, and Yaz in left. Dom DiMaggio and Fred Lynn in center, and Dwight Evans in right.

Ted would take a lot of batting practice, and he'd do a lot of hitting on an off day. He was always swinging a bat, and he had such a great mind. When we were just kids on the Red Sox, we all lived at the Sheraton Hotel on the river in Boston. Ted had a big mirror in his room, and he'd stand in front of it and look at his swing. For a guy that young, blessed with all that talent, he really worked to take advantage of it.

When I hit in front of Ted, I never got to hit 2-and-0 or 3-and-1. I had to take, hoping I could get a walk, because we never wanted Williams leading off an inning. I used to get brushed with pitches just to get him up to the plate. One time I came into the dugout after grounding to second on a 3-and-1 pitch and I said to nobody in particular, "Why don't I get to hit 2-and-0 and 3-and-1 more often." Our manager Joe McCarthy heard me and said, "As long as you're here, you'll do as you're told." I felt like a nickel. I went to see him after the game and I said, "Joe, I'm sorry." He said "I understand your frustration, but we've got the best hitter in baseball." I thought McCarthy was the smartest man I ever played for.

I remember in 1946 we got off to a great start. Dom DiMaggio was hitting .400, I was hitting .400, and Williams was hitting .500. Bobby Doerr was hitting behind Ted, and Bobby was hitting about .260. We were about 30 or 40 games into the season, and one day before batting practice, Bobby, Dom and me were in the dugout talking and here comes Ted. He says to Doerr, "For crying out loud, you got your hands up here, down here, open stance, closed stance, feet together — get a good stance and give it a try." Bobby said to him, "Ted, I'm not you." Williams threw his arms up and said, "You want to be a lousy .280 hitter, be a lousy .280 hitter." Doerr went on to knock in 116 runs that year. That was Ted — a real perfectionist when it came to hitting.

Yaz, by the time he was 25 years old, was a complete player. At first he was kind of a wild swinger. But he could hit, and he had great baseball instincts. I've heard Dick Williams say that if he had to take one year for someone who was most outstanding in everything he did, he would take Yaz in 1967. That year Yaz would hit a homer in the late innings if we were one or two runs down, or he would make a great catch, or throw someone out whatever it took. I managed Yaz in 1963 and 1964. I was energetic and young, and I felt good about managing for the club I grew up with. I made a couple of suggestions to Yaz, and he kind of barked at me a little bit. Maybe my tone of voice wasn't what it could have been. I learned from that; I found out you don't bother the good players. My first year, he was at the plate with a man on third with one out, and he decided to bunt on his own. I said "Carl, you're our best player. I'm depending on you to hit the ball. You might hit one out of the ballpark. I don't want you bunting. It would be like asking Ted Williams to bunt." I ruffled his feathers a little bit.

And let's not forget Jim Rice, one of my all-time favorites. He was a terrific hitter, so strong, power to all fields. Rice really worked at learning how to play the Wall. I hit him a lot of balls off the Wall, line drives, on the ground — and he never had enough. He'd say, "Come on Woody (short for Woodpecker, Pesky's nickname), let's go." When he first got here, he threw sidearm, but when he realized that if you throw over the top, the ball wouldn't tail, it would

go straight, he wound up leading the league in assists for outfielders.

 If you have to pick one, it's Williams. He was a great teammate, and he was one of the all-time perfectionists. If he put his mind to it, there wasn't anything he couldn't do better than the other guy. He didn't try to impress anyone; he just wanted to be the best at the things that were important to him. For example, he was nuts about fishing, and he became a great fisherman. I went with him once in Cleveland to see a guy who made flies for fishing for a living. Ted showed the guy some of the flies he had made, and the guy said, "You make them better than I do."

Yastrzemski was a leader. He was the leader of the band, like a Joe DiMaggio, one of those type guys. You couldn't wait until Yaz got to bat. He could really help you in the outfield too, especially playing balls off the Green Monster. Any ball he could get to he could catch, and he had a pretty good arm. Yaz held his bat very high when he came up, and Williams told him, "We aren't going to do any changing now, but some day we're gonna bring that bat down and you'll be in position to hit." Before you know it, Yaz did bring his bat down.

FRED LYNN

JIM RICE

[76]

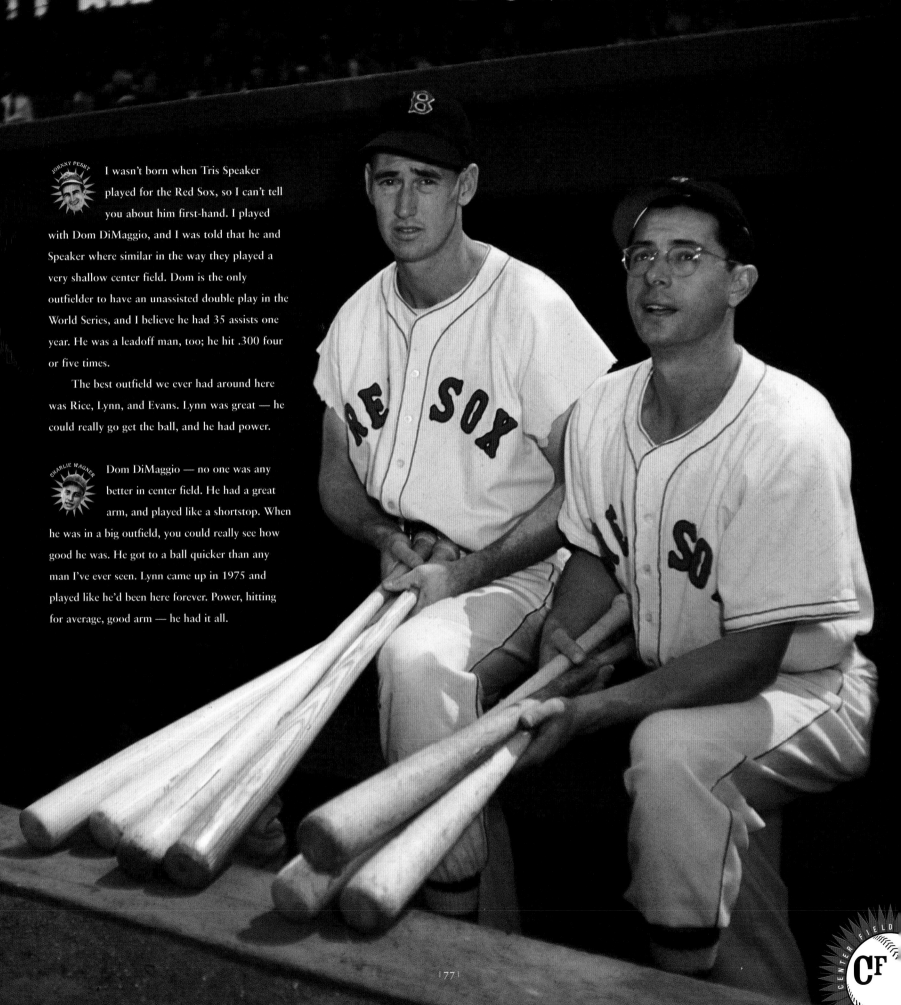

DOM DiMAGGIO

JOHNNY PESKY I wasn't born when Tris Speaker played for the Red Sox, so I can't tell you about him first-hand. I played with Dom DiMaggio, and I was told that he and Speaker where similar in the way they played a very shallow center field. Dom is the only outfielder to have an unassisted double play in the World Series, and I believe he had 35 assists one year. He was a leadoff man, too; he hit .300 four or five times.

The best outfield we ever had around here was Rice, Lynn, and Evans. Lynn was great — he could really go get the ball, and he had power.

CHARLIE WAGNER Dom DiMaggio — no one was any better in center field. He had a great arm, and played like a shortstop. When he was in a big outfield, you could really see how good he was. He got to a ball quicker than any man I've ever seen. Lynn came up in 1975 and played like he'd been here forever. Power, hitting for average, good arm — he had it all.

Dwight Evans was a big, good-looking guy, about 6-foot-3, looked like Rock Hudson. He could hit, run and throw — just a helluva player. He hit almost 400 home runs.

Evans is the best right fielder we've ever had, no question. I had him as a kid in the minors in Corning, New York, and it was just a treat to watch everything he could do. He had a great arm, and he took real pleasure in throwing the ball accurately.

DWIGHT EVANS

PEDRO MARTINEZ

JOHNNY PESKY

Roger Clemens is as good a pitcher as I've ever seen. To me he's the best pitcher the Red Sox ever had, although you'll probably get some argument from others on that. Cy Young was well before my time, but you gotta include him. The rest of my starting five is Pedro Martinez, Mel Parnell, and Tex Hughson. My reliever is Dick Radatz.

We all know how great Pedro is. Parnell was a stylish lefthander, a great pitcher. Hughson won 20, and he came up lame. We had other good ones here, too. Boo Ferriss won 21 in 1945, his first year with us, and 25 the next year, but he had an asthmatic condition. One day in Chicago in 95-degree heat, he kept having to use the inhaler he carried in his pocket, but he still went nine innings. A real tough kid. Mickey Harris and Joe Dobson showed real promise, but they both came up lame, too.

PITCHER P

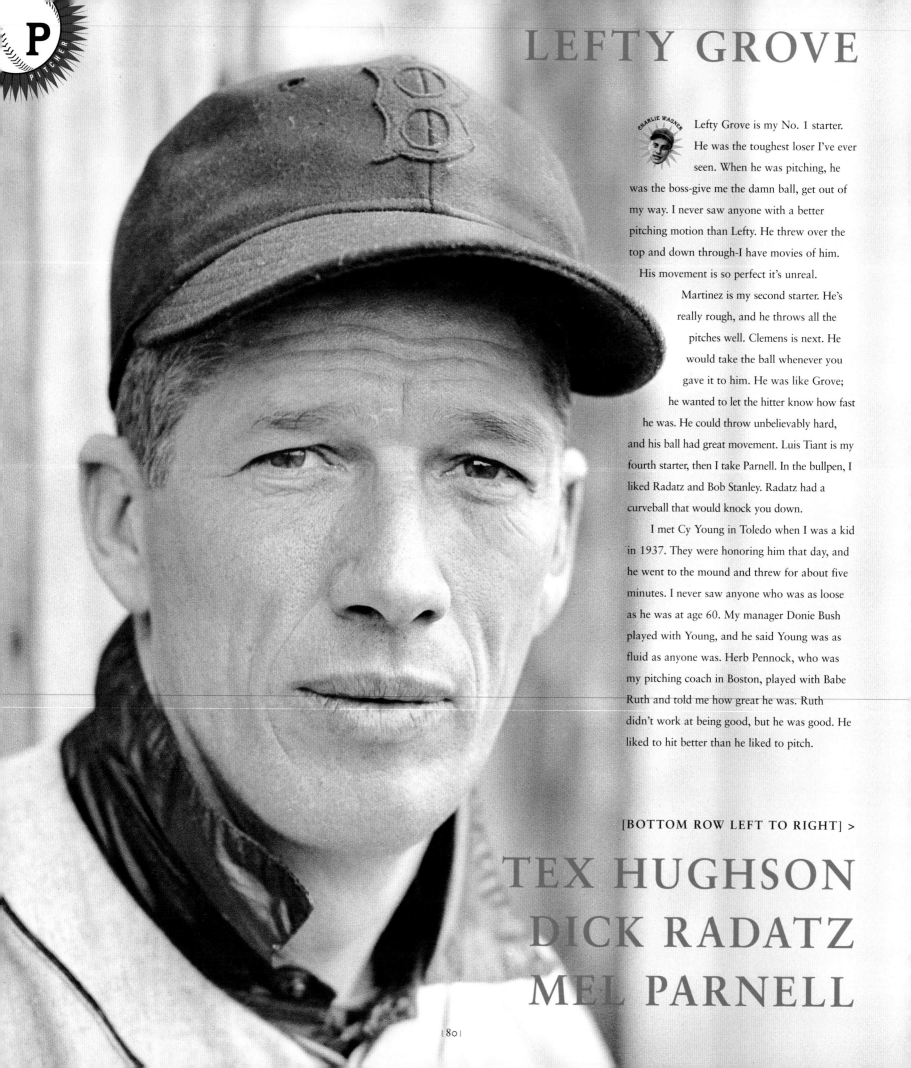

LEFTY GROVE

CHARLIE WAGNER

Lefty Grove is my No. 1 starter. He was the toughest loser I've ever seen. When he was pitching, he was the boss-give me the damn ball, get out of my way. I never saw anyone with a better pitching motion than Lefty. He threw over the top and down through-I have movies of him. His movement is so perfect it's unreal.

Martinez is my second starter. He's really rough, and he throws all the pitches well. Clemens is next. He would take the ball whenever you gave it to him. He was like Grove; he wanted to let the hitter know how fast he was. He could throw unbelievably hard, and his ball had great movement. Luis Tiant is my fourth starter, then I take Parnell. In the bullpen, I liked Radatz and Bob Stanley. Radatz had a curveball that would knock you down.

I met Cy Young in Toledo when I was a kid in 1937. They were honoring him that day, and he went to the mound and threw for about five minutes. I never saw anyone who was as loose as he was at age 60. My manager Donie Bush played with Young, and he said Young was as fluid as anyone was. Herb Pennock, who was my pitching coach in Boston, played with Babe Ruth and told me how great he was. Ruth didn't work at being good, but he was good. He liked to hit better than he liked to pitch.

[BOTTOM ROW LEFT TO RIGHT] >

TEX HUGHSON
DICK RADATZ
MEL PARNELL

ROGER CLEMENS

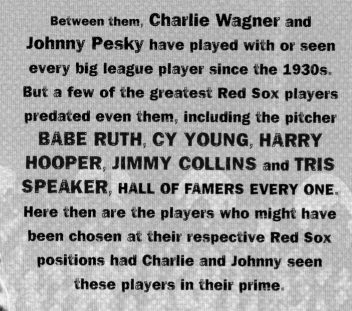

Between them, **Charlie Wagner** and **Johnny Pesky** have played with or seen every big league player since the 1930s. But a few of the greatest Red Sox players predated even them, including the pitcher **BABE RUTH, CY YOUNG, HARRY HOOPER, JIMMY COLLINS** and **TRIS SPEAKER,** HALL OF FAMERS EVERY ONE. Here then are the players who might have been chosen at their respective Red Sox positions had Charlie and Johnny seen these players in their prime.

RUTH
AS A PITCHER
IN HIS FIRST THREE FULL SEASONS
1915 - 1916 - 1917

2.02 ERA

	WINS		VICTORIES BY AGE
65		**67**	
33	LOSSES	**23**	

ONLY THREE PITCHERS IN THIS CENTURY WON MORE GAMES THAN RUTH BY AGE 23:

BOB FELLER	107
SMOKY JOE WOOD	81
DWIGHT GOODEN	73

Clearly those accomplishments present a compelling case for Ruth as the greatest hitter who ever lived. But there can be no argument that he was the greatest player ever, based on one simple fact: Given a chance, Ruth also might have become one of the game's great pitchers. Consider this: In his first three seasons, before he began the transition to outfielder, Ruth posted a record of 65-33 with a 2.02 ERA. The ERA was the fourth best in the majors during those three seasons (1915-1917) and he ranked third in victories during that span behind a pair of high-end Hall of Famers: Grover Cleveland Alexander (94-35) and Walter Johnson (75-49).

By the time he turned 23, Ruth had earned 67 victories. Only three pitchers in this century won more games by that age: Bob Feller (107), Smoky Joe Wood (81) and Dwight Gooden (73).

Generations later, it's difficult to appreciate the magnitude of Ruth's unprecedented hitting achievements, at least as they were viewed by his contemporaries. Perhaps only in recent years, as Mark McGwire stretched the limits of what many once considered possible, have we seen anything to help put Ruth in that context. But combined with what Ruth did as a pitcher, and the unrealized potential that it implied, there really is nothing before or after to compare.

116	WINS
57	LOSSES

20 WINS OR MORE IN
1911 AND 1912

WOOD

14 SEASONS
1908-1915 WITH THE RED SOX

2.03 ERA

Nobody threw harder than Smoky Joe Wood, a fact acknowledged by even the great Walter Johnson. "Can I throw harder than Joe Wood? Mister, there's no man alive can throw hard than Joe Wood," Johnson told a sports writer in 1912. The 5-feet-11-inch, 180-pound Wood enjoyed one of the greatest seasons ever by a pitcher in 1912, going 34-5 with 35 complete games and 10 shutouts, then winning three games in the World Series as the Red Sox beat the New York Giants. For good measure, Wood batted .290 in 1912. On September 6, 1912, the 22-year-old Wood and the 24-year-old Johnson engaged in one of baseball's all-time classic pitching match-ups. Wood, working on a 14-game winning streak, beat Johnson and the Washington Senators, 1-0, in a game pitched so efficiently that it was over in just 106 minutes. Wood's streak would reach 16, tying a major league record that Johnson had set earlier in the season. The following spring, Wood slipped on wet grass while fielding a ground ball and suffered a broken right thumb. When he was able to pitch again, he could not throw without experiencing pain in his right shoulder. Wood persevered and pitched for the Red Sox for three more seasons, even going 15-5 and leading the American League in ERA (1.49) in 1915. The pain, though, drove him out of baseball for a year, and when he returned he soon gave up pitching and completed his career as an outfielder with the Cleveland Indians.

20 wins or more 16 times,
30 wins or more five times

22 seasons, including 1901-1908 with the Red Sox

14 seasons, including 1901-1907 with the Red Sox

YOUNG
Cy

COLLINS
Jimmy

PITCHER
511-313 » 2.63 ERA
HALL OF FAME » 1937

THIRD BASE
.294 » 64 HR » 982 RBIs
HALL OF FAME » 1945

By the time he joined the Red Sox in 1901, Cy Young had won 286 games and pitched more than 4,000 innings — numbers that would indicate a fabulous career for 99 percent of the pitchers who have worked in the major leagues. Young was 34 at the time, and in his eight years in Boston he would win another 193 games on his way to 511 career victories — 94 more than any other pitcher in history. Remarkably, Young might have had more victories, but he grew into a portly man and opponents seized on the opportunity to regularly bunt successfully against him. So he was forced into retirement at age 44, without so much as a twinge of pain in a remarkable right arm that churned out 7,356 innings — 1,415 more than any other pitcher in history. Young attributed his good health to an offseason regime of chopping wood and doing heavy chores on his Ohio farm. Born Denton True Young, he gained his nickname from a catcher who warmed him up when he tried out for the Canton, Ohio, minor league team. The catcher told sports writers Young threw "as fast as a cyclone." So he became Cy, a pitcher with records that likely will forever remain unchallenged.

Jimmy Collins was the Red Sox's first manager and their first star player. He jumped to the team for its inaugural season in 1901 after being offered more money than Boston's National League club, the Braves, would pay him. Collins had no peer among third basemen until Pie Traynor came along in the 1920s. Sturdily built at 5-feet, 8-inches and 160 pounds, Collins was a fine hitter (better than .300 five times) and had above-average power for his day. While he was a true asset at the plate, his value soared once he took his defensive position. Sure-handed and ultra-quick, Collins was a master at fielding bunts, which were a frequent offensive ploy in the dead-ball era. He holds the National League record for chances by a third baseman in a season (601 in 1899) and ranks second all-time at his position in career putouts. Collins was the Red Sox's manager for six years, including the pennant-winning seasons of 1903 and 1904. The Red Sox won the first World Series, in 1903, but there was no Series in 1904 because the leagues were feuding. Collins was traded to the Philadelphia Athletics in 1908 and was out of baseball by 1911. He was inducted into the Hall of Fame in 1945, two years after his death at age 69 in his native Buffalo, New York.

22 seasons, including 1907-15 with the Red Sox

17 seasons, including 1909-1920 with the Red Sox

SPEAKER *Tris*

HOOPER *Harry*

CENTER FIELD

.344 » 117 HR » 1,881 RBIs

HALL OF FAME » 1937

RIGHT FIELD

.281 » 75 HR » 817 RBIs

HALL OF FAME » 1971

By most accounts, Tris Speaker was one of the top 10 players among those in the major leagues during the first half of the 20th century. His plaque in the Hall of Fame describes him as the greatest center fielder of his day. From 1910 to 1915, Speaker, Harry Hooper and Duffy Lewis formed the Red Sox's famed "Million Dollar Outfield." One of the fastest players of his era, Speaker played shallow in center field, daring batters to try and hit the ball over his head; they rarely did. The 6-foot, 195-pound Speaker had a powerful swing from the left side of the plate that rained line drives to all fields. More than 70 years after he ceased playing, he remains the all-time major league leader for doubles (793). Hugely popular in Boston, Speaker was one of the first athletes to cash in on his celebrity. He received $50 each time he hit the Bull Durham sign at Fenway Park, endorsed Boston Garters, had a $2 straw hat named in his honor, and received free clothing from manufacturers. The Texas-born Speaker would have been content to spend his career in Boston if not for the slight he felt when Red Sox owner Joe Lannin attempted to cut his salary to less than $10,000 after the club won the 1915 World Series. Lannin cited Speaker's batting average, which had fallen for four straight seasons. Speaker refused to sign and was traded to the Cleveland Indians, who benefited from his .354 batting average over the next 11 seasons. It was the second time the Red Sox had infuriated Speaker. Trying to make the team as a 20-year-old in 1908, he did not fare well in spring training and was left behind in Little Rock, Arkansas, as payment for the use of the training camp.

Although he was a fine ballplayer as part of the Red Sox's "Million Dollar Outfield" with Tris Speaker and Duffy Lewis, Harry Hooper is best-remembered for his part in Babe Ruth leaving the pitcher's mound for full-time work as a hitter. As the story goes, the erudite Hooper — he was a college man — convinced Red Sox manager Ed Barrow that as great as the young Ruth was on the mound, he had even more promise as a hitter. Barrow agreed to let Ruth play in the outfield on the days he didn't pitch. The left-handed batting Hooper was the Red Sox's leadoff hitter and right fielder from 1909 through 1920. He got on base more than 40 percent of the time and ran the bases better than any of his teammates. When he left the Red Sox, he was the club's all-time leader in triples (130) and stolen bases (300). Hooper was an innovator in the outfield, developing the rump slide to catch short fly balls that became widely copied, and he had a rifle for an arm. The California native was inducted into the Hall of Fame in 1971 and he died three years later at age 87.

1967

AQUARIUS DAWNED, BOSTON ROCKED, AND ALL HELL BROKE LOOSE

NINETEEN SIXTY-SEVEN

THE MOON WAS IN THE SEVENTH HOUSE.

Yaz batted third.

JUPITER ALIGNED WITH MARS.

Lonborg faced Chance.

PEACE GUIDED THE PLANETS.

BUT ROXBURY BURNED, AND VIETNAM WAS DEATH.

Dick Williams raged.

In 1967 Aquarius dawned, Boston rocked and all hell broke loose. More American soldiers died in Vietnam by the end of September — 6,721 — than during the previous six years. Heavyweight champion Muhammad Ali was stripped of his title for refusing a draft notice. Israel repulsed Arab armies in a six-day war. Former Harvard professor Timothy Leary preached the virtue of hallucinogenic drugs. Georgetown undergraduate Bill Clinton smoked pot but didn't inhale. Jimi Hendrix lit his Fender Stratocaster on fire at the Monterey Pop Festival. Black ghettos ignited with frustration and rage. The Beatles meditated with Maharishi Mahesh Yogi while flower children went to San Francisco for a Summer of Love. Martin Luther King Jr. and Bobby Kennedy were alive, and so were J. Edgar Hoover and George Wallace. Richard Nixon was planning his comeback, LBJ his exit.

And the Red Sox won the pennant.

It was a pennant befitting 1967, a 500-year-flood of a pennant, a pennant so frenetic and outlandish and magical it was dubbed "The Impossible Dream" after a song in a then-popular Broadway musical about Don Quixote. And really, what better imagery to describe those 100-to-1-shot Red Sox, a group that tilted at windmills and won.

Four teams — Boston, Minnesota, Chicago and Detroit — entered the final week separated by 1½ games. It ended on the final evening of the final day, with the Red Sox glued to a clubhouse radio, listening as the California Angels eliminated the Tigers in the second game of a doubleheader at Detroit.

Power to the people of Red Sox Nation!

Nobody gave the Red Sox a chance, except perhaps the 8,324 fans who showed up for Opening Day at Fenway Park for a 5-4 win over the White Sox. By the middle of the summer, and in ensuing years as attendance swelled toward 1.7 million, 8,324 would seem as

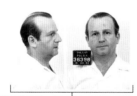

1967 >

01.03.67

> Jack Ruby, assassin of Lee Harvey Oswald, dies at the age of 55.

[88]

obsolete as the dreary era preceding it. From 1960 through 1966 the Red Sox lost 125 games more than they won and never finished higher than sixth place. In 1965 they were ninth with a 62-100 record, and in 1966 they were ninth again at 72-90 with home attendance of 811,172. The Red Sox were called everything in those days, including selfish, lazy and spoiled. But Red Sox owner Tom Yawkey set a new direction in late 1965 with the promotion of his business manager, Dick O'Connell, to general manager. In turn, he hired rookie manager, Dick Williams, to lead the charge into 1967.

The 37-year-old Williams became the second-youngest manager in the major leagues, and probably the most surly and sarcastic. Crewcut and authoritarian, he was the drill sergeant nightmare of every hippie, and the scourge of laid-back baseball. Having ended his journeyman career on the 1963 and 1964 Boston squads, Williams was on to the tricks of his former teammates. "They knew what I knew," Williams says. "They had been goofing off and stealing Mr. Yawkey's money." Williams motivated with the spur and whip-what he couldn't accomplish with criticism and threats he did with fines and benchings. He lumped players together with umpires, reporters and league officials — treating them all the same, which was badly.

In his 1990 autobiography, *No More Mr. Nice Guy*, Williams recounted his hardscrabble St. Louis childhood and a tough-as-nails but oft-unemployed father. Williams learned to swim when his father tossed him in the rushing current of an Ozark river, ordered him to stroke, and stood behind him while the current forced him downstream. This harsh upbringing shaped his managing, Williams wrote, because "my competitive fire, kindled in me during those days of learning to swim upstream in a Missouri river, became a continuous rolling explosion. If we lost and we'd done everything right, I'd try to understand. It would be painful but I'd try. But if we lost because one person had made a mental mistake, I'd blow up. Sometimes right on the spot, even before the game was won or lost — if I thought somebody didn't care as much as I did, I'd damn near kill him."

In February 1967, this was the authoritative personality confronting a group of players described by a newspaper reporter as "a pack of rookies, misfits, castoffs and Carl Yastrzemski." Surely pitcher Jim Lonborg, first baseman George Scott, second baseman Mike Andrews, shortstop Rico Petrocelli, and outfielders Tony Conigliaro and Reggie Smith merited greater respect. But the basic premise was sound-Yastrzemski was lead dog. A six-year veteran and former batting champion, Yaz was a good player falling short of

> Albert DeSalvo, the Boston Strangler, is sentenced to life in prison.

01.18.67

01.23.67

The Red Sox report they have received an offer of $500,000 from the Athletics for 22-year-old outfielder Tony Conigliaro.

DALTON JONES

greatness. His outward lack of emotion occasionally appeared like nonchalance, and his close relationship with Yawkey had cut the legs out from under a couple of managers.

Moving quickly to assert control, Williams stripped Yaz of his captaincy and replaced him with ... himself. Henceforth there would be no captain, Williams announced, because anyone with a problem or complaint could bring it to him directly. The unspoken message was that everyone from star to journeyman would be treated alike. (How iconoclastic was the manager? Early in spring training another Williams — the legendary Ted — showed up, as he had routinely since his retirement, to lecture on the finer points of the game. When Ted disagreed with some of Dick's methods, specifically having pitchers play volleyball to improve their eye-hand coordination, Dick told Ted to stay away from his pitchers and his pitchers to stay away from Ted; soon, Ted stayed away from Dick, packed up and left.)

Williams set up a weight chart and instituted daily weigh-ins. (This proved to be a season-long problem for the plumpish Scott, an avid and capable eater, until Williams finally benched him for a three-game series with the Angels in August. From then on, Scott made his weight.) When two players showed up late for a spring training workout, Williams publicly berated them and ordered the team hotel to call the rooms of all players at 7 a.m. each day. Training camp was a refresher course on fundamentals —

principles Williams had learned coming up in the Los Angeles Dodgers system. "Right from the start you could see he meant business," Petrocelli says. "He got on people for mental mistakes. He could tolerate an error, but not a mental mistake. You had to be in the game."

Williams also could delegate authority judiciously. Petrocelli, the third-year shortstop, had lost his confidence under the previous manager, Billy Herman. Williams set about restoring it by telling Petrocelli he was in charge of the young infield of third baseman Joe Foy, second baseman Mike Andrews and Scott. "If you want to move these guys around, you don't have to ask me," Williams told Petrocelli.

"I like it," the shortstop replied. The ripple effect had Andrews, a rookie, improving under Petrocelli's guidance. "I had only played one season at second in the minors," Andrews says. "But Rico was so steady he made it work."

A disciplined and businesslike club opened the season, and in the third game an omen was delivered. Rookie lefthander Billy Rohr came within one out of pitching a no-hitter against the New York Yankees at Yankee Stadium. Yastrzemski kept it alive with a spectacular tumbling catch of a Tom Tresh smash to open the ninth, but with two out Elston Howard lined a clean single to right. Rohr pocketed the one-hit 3-0 shutout, and even though he won just one more game and faded back to the minors, his cameo was a precursor to the Impossible Dream.

 US troops begin largest offensive of the Vietnam War

02.23.67

03.06.67

03.31.67

Teamster boss Jimmy Hoffa enters Lewisburg Federal Prison

In London, Jimi Hendrix set his guitar on fire for the first time

1967 BATTING AVERAGE
.303

RUNS
74

DOUBLES
21

GEORGE [**BOOMER**] SCOTT

HOME RUNS
19

RBI
82

FIELDING PERCENTAGE
.987

"If I thought somebody didn't care as much as I did, I'd damn near kill him."

DICK WILLIAMS

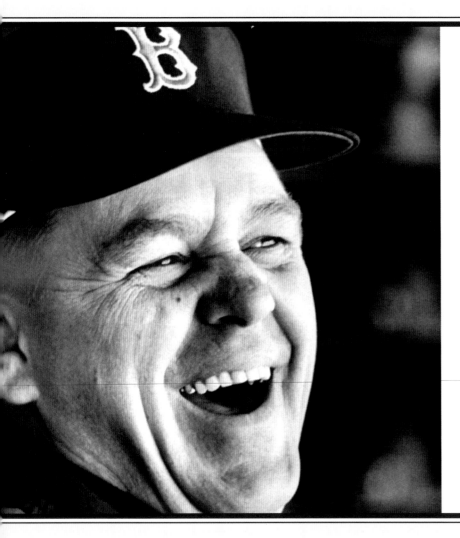

As April and May unfolded, Williams was unrelenting, not only with his players, but with umpires. Slumping players — among them Yastrzemski, Smith, Scott and Foy — were benched. Yawkey, whose presence in the clubhouse Williams viewed as subversive, was given the cold shoulder. Williams' baiting of umpires was obsessive and nasty-in one game he argued with umpires at first base, second, third and home plate. Yet the manager's aggressiveness transformed righthander Jim Lonborg, whose Stanford pedigree reflected a genteel manner on the mound, as did his 19-27 career record. Williams ordered Lonborg to pitch inside and to use his hard sinking fastball in tight situations. In a May game against the Angels, Lonborg took a 1-0 lead into the bottom of the ninth and blew it, 2-1, trying to finesse batters. "As Jim is walking off, Rico Petrocelli patted him on the back and said 'nice game' to bolster him," says Red Sox radio broadcaster Ken Coleman. "Dick Williams overheard it and said 'nice game, my ass.'"

Lonborg got the message. In June, after Foy was beaned by the Yankees' Thad Tillotson, Lonborg drilled Tillotson in the shoulder, inciting a brawl. When Lonborg came to bat, Tillotson plunked him, and the clubs brawled again. Lonborg retaliated by hitting Dick Howser in the back, clearing the benches a third time. Williams and Yankees manager Ralph Houk were threatened with suspensions, but Williams was exhilarated. "In that one incident [Lonborg] had proved

 New Zealander Dave McKenzie won the Boston Marathon, setting a course record of 2:15:45.

04.14.67

04.19.67

At Yankee Stadium, lefthander Bill Rohr makes his major league debut for the Red Sox, no-hitting New York for 8⅔ innings.

to me and to the rest of the league that he wasn't going to be just another frightened kid with talent — he was going to be a scary kid with talent," Williams wrote.

With the unwanted burden of being captain lifted, Yaz set about finding his inner Hall of Famer. Batting coach Bobby Doerr got Yaz to hold his bat high, and with his new stance he was consistently able to turn on the ball and pull it high and deep to right. In June, White Sox manager Eddie Stanky commented that Yaz was an All-Star "from the neck down." In a doubleheader the following day Yaz went 6 for 9 and homered in his final at-bat. As he headed for home Yaz tipped his cap to Stanky. Of Williams, Yastrzemski later would say, "He was the right guy at the time. He was young, aggressive, full of fire. Personally, I liked him. I know what he was trying to do. But he might have been a little harsh at times."

By the end of May the Red Sox were two games above .500 and not yet a contender. O'Connell made a couple of smart moves in early June, acquiring utility infielder Jerry Adair from the White Sox and righthander Gary Bell from the Cleveland Indians. Also in June, Conigliaro stunned the White Sox, 2-1, with a two-out, two-run home run on a 3-and-2 pitch in the bottom of the eleventh; at the end of the month Boston was three games over .500, 5½ games behind Chicago. At the All-Star break the Sox were six games out. The break provided a barometer. The reborn Lonborg, who had mounted a 10-2 record, and Yastrzemski, Petrocelli and Conigliaro went to the midsummer classic. "About halfway through the year we realized, 'Hey, there's no one better than us out there,'" Andrews says. "We had so many young guys. Once we'd been around the league we knew how good we were."

After the break the Red Sox jelled dramatically, winning 10 in a row, improving to 52-40 and pulling to within a half-game of the White Sox. Arriving back at Boston's Logan Airport on July 23 the Sox were greeted by 10,000 madly screaming fans-more than had attended Opening Day. "You'd have thought the Beatles landed," Petrocelli says. Fans and players mingled at the baggage carousel — floating on a cloud of baseball euphoria. That moment may pinpoint the birth of modern Red Sox Nation. New England throbbed with pennant fever. Ken Coleman's children were at crowded Nantasket Beach on a steamy Sunday afternoon when the Sox fell behind the Angels, 8-0. Thousands of transistor radios crackled as the Sox mounted a comeback. Adair won the game, 9-8, with a walk-off home run. "My kids told me the beach erupted-a hundred thousand people were screaming," Coleman says.

They were dancing on Nantasket Beach, and in the streets, and all along the watchtower. The pulse of Red Sox Nation quickened.

04.28.67

 Muhammad Ali is stripped of his boxing title after refusing induction into the Army.

[PUTOUTS + ASSISTS] ÷ [PUTOUTS + ASSISTS + ERRORS] =

.970

1967 FIELDING PERCENTAGE [**RICO PETROCELLI**]

Yet baseball's bubble existence could not keep out the larger world. The Red Sox often shared Page One with stark headlines:

"19 Year Olds First, Draft Chief Says"

Four players — Lonborg, Conigliaro, Dalton Jones and Jim Landis — were called for two-week stints with their reserve military units. Letters from Vietnam routinely arrived in the clubhouse. Soldiers were listening to Red Sox broadcasts on Armed Forces Radio. "I pray to God I live long enough to see you guys win the pennant," wrote a soldier. Petrocelli shudders remembering those letters. "We were aware of what was happening," he says. "We were concerned." Andrews visited wounded soldiers recuperating at a military hospital in the Charlestown neighborhood of Boston. "This chaotic war was going on while we were playing baseball," Andrews says. "To think that baseball could be meaningful to these wounded soldiers was unbelievable."

Early in June came another headline:

"Police Battle Rioters in Roxbury"

Boston's poorest and blackest neighborhood erupted in flames. A firefighter was shot in the wrist by a sniper. Detroit was rioting when the Red Sox arrived for a three-game series. "There was shooting down the street from Tiger Stadium," Petrocelli says. "We took the bus from the ballpark to the hotel. We couldn't go out of the hotel." America was tearing apart at the seams. Or was it simply molting a cancerous skin?

Within baseball itself a revolution was sprouting. A new and aggressive executive director of the Major League Baseball Players Association, Marvin Miller, was setting his sights on the feudal control exercised by owners. With the overturning of the illegal reserve clause his ultimate objective — to be achieved in 1975 — Miller pushed for improvements in pension benefits, minimum salary, and working conditions. Documenting the embryonic union movement in 1967, author John Helyar wrote that one player representative, pitcher Milt Pappas, even spoke up for the growing ranks of players abandoning crewcuts for the mod look. "There aren't enough outlets for hair dryers in the clubhouses," Pappas complained.

05.01.67

 Singer Elvis Presley weds Priscilla Ann Beaulieu in Las Vegas.

05.05.67

Facing the Orioles' Eddie Fisher, Carl Yastrzemski hits his 100th career home run at Fenway Park.

"Sub-Culture of Hippies Linked to Red Threat in U.S."

A gathering of ultra-conservatives calling itself the New England Rally for God, Family and Country met at the Statler Hilton. The organizer proclaimed that "the breakdown of law and order, emergence of narcotics as a significant peril, burgeoning of the New Left on campuses and folk songs and folk singers, are all tied to a breakdown of morality and faith effected by communists in America." A culture was emerging, all right, and some rushed to embrace it. A new publication, Avante-Garde Magazine, introduced itself as "a forward-looking daring and wildly hedonistic magazine… It will be the voice of the Turned-On Generation."

That "turned-on" generation, high school and college students, was going to Fenway by the thousands, filling the $2 bleacher seats, getting high on its first pennant race.

Sox fans, shivering and wrapped in blankets play a game of chess while they wait in line outside Fenway Park to buy tickets for the 1967 World Series.

> Keith Richards, Brian Jones, and Mick Jagger of the Rolling Stones are arrested on drug charges.

> In a case of tragic "misidentification" Israel downs USS Liberty in Mediterranean, killing 34 US crewmen.

05.10.67   05.17.67   06.08.67   06.12.67

> The Orioles and Red Sox play long ball with 10 home runs in a 12-8 Baltimore victory.

> Supreme Court unanimously overturns laws that ban interracial marriages.

[CARL YASTRZEMSKI]

1967
Triple Crown Winner

THE YEAR OF YAZ

LEAGUE LEADER
BATTING AVERAGE • RBI • HOME RUNS

Yastrzemski kicked into overdrive, on his way to a Triple Crown season of which the figures (.326, 44 homers, 121 RBI) merely hint at his impact. The Red Sox won 16 of their final 27 games, a stretch in which Yaz went 40 for 96 (.417), driving in 26 runs and scoring 24.

BATTING AVERAGE		RUNS BATTED IN		HOME RUNS	
Yastrzemski-Bos	.326	Yastrzemski-Bos	121	Yastrzemski-Bos	44
F.Robinson-Bal	.311	F.Robinson-Bal	113	Killebrew-Min	44
Kaline-Det	.308	Killebrew-Min	94	Howard-Was	36
Scott-Bos	.303	Howard-Was	89	F.Robinson-Bal	30
Blair-Bal	.293	Oliva-Min	83		

RUNS		RUNS PRODUCED		DOUBLES	
Yastrzemski-Bos	112	Yastrzemski-Bos	189	Oliva-Min	34
Killebrew-Min	105	Killebrew-Min	174	Tovar-Min	32
Tovar-Min	98	F.Robinson-Bal	147	Yastrzemski-Bos	31
Kaline-Det	94	Kaline-Det	147	D.Johnson-Bal	30
McAuliffe-Det	92	B.Robinson-Bal	143	Campaneris-KC	29

BASE ON BALLS		ON BASE PERCENTAGE		SLUGGING AVERAGE	
Killebrew-Min	131	Yastrzemski-Bos	.421	Yastrzemski-Bos	.622
Mantle-NY	107	Kaline-Det	.415	F.Robinson-Bal	.576
McAuliffe-Det	105	Killebrew-Min	.413	Killebrew-Min	.558
Yastrzemski-Bos	91	F.Robinson-Bal	.408	Kaline-Det	.541
Kaline-Det	83	Mantle-NY	.394	Howard-Was	.511

HITS		TOTAL BASES		TOTAL PLAYER RATING	
Yastrzemski-Bos	189	Yastrzemski-Bos	360	Yastrzemski-Bos	7.3
Tovar-Min	173	Killebrew-Min	305	Kaline-Det	5.2
Scott-Bos	171	F.Robinson-Bal	276	B.Robinson-Bal	5.0
Fregosi-Cal	171	B.Robinson-Bal	265	F.Robinson-Bal	4.8
B.Robinson-Bal	164	Howard-Was	265	Blair-Bal	4.1

"THE IMPOSSIBLE DREAM"

Four teams — Boston, Minnesota, Chicago and Detroit — entered the final week separated by 1½ games. It ended on the final evening of the final day, with the Red Sox glued to a clubhouse radio, listening as the California Angels eliminated the Tigers in the second game of a doubleheader at Detroit.

On August 18, tragedy struck. Conigliaro was beaned by Angels righthander Jack Hamilton. The pitch busted up the left side of Conigliaro's face, damaged his vision, and nearly killed him. Conigliaro's season-ending injury cost the Red Sox their cleanup hitter. O'Connell moved decisively, signing power hitter Ken "Hawk" Harrelson, a flamboyant and independent soul who, perhaps more than any major leaguer, personified the turbulent year.

Harrelson had been released by Kansas City Athletics owner Charlie Finley for, essentially, refusing to be subservient. Finley fined Harrelson for throwing baseballs to fans, wearing his socks the wrong way, and assorted other acts of defiance. Finally, after Finley fined a teammate for drinking on a flight, Harrelson had had enough and blasted Finley in the newspapers, calling him a "menace" to baseball and "detrimental" to the game. Outraged, Finley released Harrelson. Thus Harrelson was a free agent (albeit a worried one) when O'Connell called and offered him a jaw-dropping three-year, $450,000 contract. At the time Yastrzemski was the club's highest-paid player at $50,000; the total payroll was $825,000. Average major league salary in 1967 was $19,000; minimum was $6,000, only $1,000 more than in 1947.

The day Harrelson reported, his wardrobe of Nehru jackets in tow, two games separated the four contenders. On September 1, Harrelson had three hits and four RBIs in a 10-2 win over the White Sox. A standing-room crowd of 34,054 (Fenway sellouts now were commonplace) saw Jose Santiago pitch the Red Sox to a half-game lead over the Twins. On September 7 all four teams were tied for first place, separated by one percentage point.

Yastrzemski kicked into overdrive, on his way to a Triple Crown season of which the figures (.326, 44 homers, 121 RBIs) merely hint at his impact. The Red Sox won 16 of their final 27 games, a stretch in which Yaz went 40 for 96 (.417), drove in 26 runs, and scored 24.

But nobody was folding. Minnesota rode the arms of Dean Chance and Jim Kaat and the bats of Harmon Killebrew, Tony Oliva and Rookie of the Year Rod Carew. Detroit's lineup included Al Kaline, Willie Horton and Bill Freehan, and a strong rotation with Mickey Lolich, Denny McLain and Earl Wilson (a former Red Sox pitcher on his way to a career-high 22 victories). The White Sox,

 Thad Tillotson hits Joe Foy of the Red Sox in the head and Jim Lonborg retaliates by hitting Tillotson. The Yankees pitcher throws at Lonborg. In the next inning, Dick Howser is hit in the head by Lonborg. It takes a dozen security officers to break up the ensuing brawl.

06.21.67

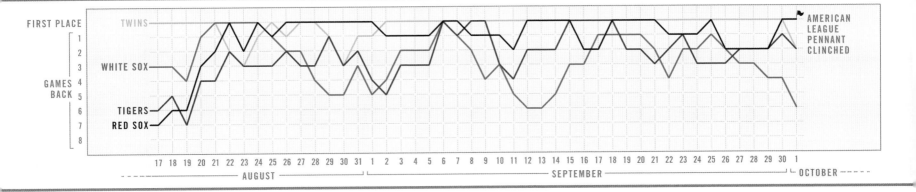

FIRST PLACE
TWINS
1
2
3
WHITE SOX
GAMES 4
BACK 5
6 TIGERS
7 RED SOX
8

AMERICAN
LEAGUE
PENNANT
CLINCHED

17 18 19 20 21 22 23 24 25 26 27 28 29 30 31 1 2 3 4 5 6 7 8 9 10 11 12 13 14 15 16 17 18 19 20 21 22 23 24 25 26 27 28 29 30 1

───── AUGUST ─────   ─────────── SEPTEMBER ─────────────   └─ OCTOBER ────┘

hitless wonders, did it with pitching: starters Joel Horlen, Gary Peters, and Tommy John and knuckleball relievers Wilbur Wood and Hoyt Wilhelm helped compile a 2.45 team ERA, the lowest since 1919.

On September 15, the Red Sox, Twins, and Tigers were tied for first at 84-64, with the White Sox 1½ back at 83-66. On September 18 in Detroit, Yastrzemski's one-out shot into the upper deck tied the game in the ninth inning, and Dalton Jones won it, 6-5, with a home run off Mike Marshall in the 10th. The Red Sox beat the Tigers the next night, 4-2, with three runs in the ninth. Cardiac Kids, indeed. "For me, it was less pressure," Yastrzemski told writer Peter Gammons. "Before that, we'd have 8,000 people in the stands, and they all wanted to see a home run or a base hit. In 1967, if you made one good defensive play, they'd give you a standing ovation."

Entering the final week the Twins had a half-game lead over the White Sox, and a one-game lead over the Tigers and Red Sox. The schedule favored the White Sox, who had two games with the last-place Athletics, and three games with the seventh-place Senators.

On Wednesday, September 27, the White Sox played a doubleheader in Kansas City while the Red Sox were off. Williams

was desperate to hear the White Sox broadcast. "I took a six-pack of Miller beer and I climbed in the front seat of my car in the parking lot of my apartment building," Williams wrote. "There I sat through the evening and into the night, hoping and willing and wishing the White Sox to lose both games before I went nuts or my car battery died." The White Sox were swept by the A's, and two days later they were eliminated with a 1-0 loss to Washington.

One by one, the contenders unraveled. The Twins dropped two of three to the fifth-place Angels, while the Tigers split two games with the ninth-place Yankees. Meanwhile at Fenway, the Red Sox lost two to the eighth-place Indians — sending New England into a miserable funk.

On Saturday morning the Twins held a one-game lead over the Red Sox and Tigers. The Tigers, at home, faced back-to-back doubleheaders with the Angels, while the Twins arrived at Fenway for two.

"We would get to play the best to become the best — I couldn't wait," Williams wrote. "To me, it was almost like the World Series come early."

In the fourth inning at Fenway Park, Angels pitcher Jack Hamilton hits Tony Conigliaro in the face with a pitch, breaking his cheekbone and sending bone fragments into his eye. The 22-year-old Conigliaro is carried off the field and taken to Sancta Maria Hospital.

07.22.67   08.18.67

Nationally renowned poet and author
Carl Sandburg dies at the age of 89.

Politicians and big-wigs elbowed for tickets. Minnesota Sen. Hubert Humphrey attended the weekend series as the guest of Massachusetts Sen. Edward Kennedy. On Saturday, Santiago pitched against Jim Kaat, who was pitching superbly until being forced to leave after suffering an elbow injury in the third inning. The Sox took a 2-1 lead in the fifth when reliever Jim Perry failed to cover first on a bad-hop grounder to the right side. Scott's 450-foot home run produced a 3-2 lead in the sixth.

Just before Scott connected, a station wagon knocked the rear bumper off a taxicab on Tremont Street at Boston Common. As reported in the Boston Herald Traveler, the "red-faced cigar-chewing" cabbie charged out of his vehicle and accosted the driver of the station wagon. But as the cabbie started to vent his spleen he overheard the radio inside the station wagon. "Scott hit a home run!," the cabbie shouted. Hostilities ceased.

The newspaper also reported the experience of a Red Line carman, Tom Kennedy, who was on duty but listening to his transistor radio during the game. Kennedy's radio lost reception when the subway car went underground. "We were ahead going into one tunnel and when we came up the score was tied," Kennedy complained. Passengers were glued to his radio. "One guy missed two stops," Kennedy said.

In the seventh Yaz hammered a three-run homer, his 44th, inducing delirium. Killebrew answered with his 44th home run in the ninth, but the Sox held on for a 6-4 win. The unsung Santiago (12-4) allowed just two hits in seven innings. In Detroit, the Tigers split, leaving them a half-game back of the Red Sox and Twins.

Sunday was for everything, with Lonborg facing Chance, and the Tigers and Angels again playing two. Williams doubted the arm-weary Tigers could sweep; he thought the winner of the Red Sox-Twins game would own the pennant. Chance (20-13) had beaten the Sox four times that season, dominating them with a sharp sinker. Lonborg (21-9) was 0-6 lifetime against the Twins.

Chance dominated the first five innings and took a 2-0 lead into the bottom of the sixth. With Lonborg due to lead off, all eyes were on Williams. "Some thought I might send up a pinch-hitter for him," Williams wrote. "But he had become one of my toughest and smartest players, and if anyone could figure out a way to pull our ass out of the sling..." Lonborg bunted Chance's first pitch, surprising third baseman Cesar Tovar, and legged out a single. Singles by Adair and Jones loaded the bases for Yastrzemski, who automatically-rapped a two-run single up the middle. A missed fielder's choice drove Chance from the mound, after which two wild pitches and an error put the Sox up, 5-2. That was all Lonborg needed.

Yaz cut short a Twins rally in the eighth by throwing out Bob Allison at second. When Petrocelli cradled a popup for the final out, fans surged onto the field and hoisted Lonborg, who happily bobbed upon a sea of shoulders. Long after the others, Lonborg appeared in the clubhouse, his uniform in tatters.

"It was great, then all of a sudden, it was terrifying," Lonborg told historian George Sullivan. "They were taking off my clothes. Somebody even took off my shoelace without taking off my shoe."

Champagne, however, remained on ice. The Tigers had won their first game, and if they won the second there would be a one-game playoff in Detroit the next day. But Denny McLain, on a sore ankle, could not hold a 3-1 lead and the Tigers trailed, 8-3, coming to bat in the bottom of the ninth. They cut the margin to 8-5 and put two runners on base with one out. With the Red Sox paralyzed in the clubhouse, and Williams listening in Yawkey's office, Dick McAuliffe rapped into a double play-ending the legendary pennant race.

Williams shouted, "It's over! It's over! It's over!" Yawkey, who hadn't touched liquor in years, raised a glass of champagne and toasted his belligerent manager. "I will drink to you," Yawkey said. Then he started to cry. Later, he embraced Yastrzemski and doubled his salary to $100,000 on the spot.

⚾ Red Sox take the first game against the Yankees, 2-1, in nine innings, Yanks win the second game in 20 innings 4-3 — a total of eight hours, 19 minutes.

08.28.67

08.29.67

⚾ Ken "Hawk" Harrelson, released by Charles O. Finley for calling the Kansas City owner "detrimental to baseball" and refusing to retract the statement, is signed by the Red Sox.

"By the dawn's early light"
Young Red Sox fans sit atop a billboard at Fenway Park and await the start of the 1967 World Series.

WINS

22

[tied for first]

WIN PERCENTAGE

.710

[second]

COMPLETE GAMES

15

[second]

INNINGS PITCHED

273

[second]

BASE ON BALLS

83

"It was great, then all of a sudden, it was terrifying. They were taking off my clothes. Somebody even took off my shoelace without taking off my shoe."

[JIM LONBORG] 1967 CY YOUNG AWARD WINNER

STRIKEOUTS

246

[first]

STRIKEOUTS/PER 9 INNINGS

8.10

[fourth]

EARNED RUN AVERAGE

3.16

SHUTOUTS

2

Jim Lonborg beats the visiting Twins, 5-3, in the final game of the year, and the Angels beat the Tigers, 8-5, to give the Red Sox the AL pennant — their first since 1946.

10.01.67

10.02.67

Thurgood Marshall, nominated by President Lyndon B. Johnson, is sworn in as the first black Supreme Court Justice.

The World Series was anticlimactic from New England's perspective. The heavily favored St. Louis Cardinals, winners of 101 games, were not swallowing the Impossible Dream. The Cardinals were fresh, and intimidating righthander Bob Gibson was at his Hall of Fame peak.

The Series belonged to Gibson. He pitched three complete games, struck out 26, and allowed just three runs. Lonborg countered with one-hit and three-hit gems. Yastrzemski hit .400, going 10 for 25 with three homers and five RBIs. In Game Seven at Fenway, Lonborg pitched on two days rest and was hammered for 10 hits and seven runs — Williams left him in at least one inning too long — in a 7-2 loss. Gibson was overpowering. "I don't think we woke up to the fact that we were in the Series until we were halfway through it," Andrews says.

Losing the Series was but a minor disappointment to most. Yastrzemski was voted the American League MVP, and Lonborg won the AL Cy Young Award.

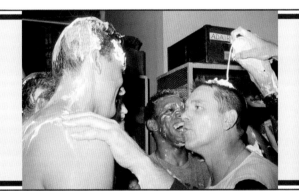 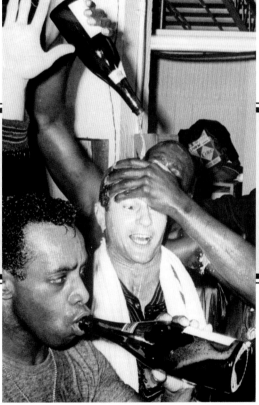 

Williams was Manager of the Year, and O'Connell won the award for top executive. History remembers the 1967 Red Sox not as a great team, but as a great story.

They were a product of their moment in time, capturing the idealism and hubris of the 1960s, a we-can-change-the-world ethos scorning convention and established hierarchy. A 100-1 longshot winning the pennant? What next? An anti-war movement toppling a president? Gender equality? Environmental awareness? Racial tolerance? A man on the moon?

"It was such an exciting and chaotic time," Andrews says. "Everything was changing. Who can say? Maybe we fed into that as a team."

Petrocelli can't go a day without someone wanting to talk about the Impossible Dream. The strangers might have been 6 or 60 that season, but they all share the same sensation: "I remember it," they say, "like it was yesterday."

In Game Six of the World Series, the Red Sox set a Series record by hitting three home runs in one inning. Boston won, 8-4.

Boston's Carl Yastrzemski is named AL MVP.

10.11.67   10.12.67   11.03.67   11.15.67

Bob Gibson three-hits the Red Sox, 7-2, in Game Seven of the World Series.

Boston's Jim Lonborg is named AL Cy Young Award winner.

The Rivalry

THE YANKEES AND THE RED SOX

BOSTON RED SOX VS. NEW YORK YANKEES

"*Whenever the Red Sox prepared to play the Yankees, it was as if they were dressing up for battle ... Against the Yankees we would button up differently, taking a little longer than usual to put on the uniform. We knew we were getting ready to take the field and uphold our values. It was as though we were knights in armor.*"

BILL LEE, *THE WRONG STUFF*

When it comes to just plain enmity, Athens and Sparta, the Capulets and the Montagues, the Hatfields and the McCoys don't have anything on the New York Yankees and Boston Red Sox. Haul out what verbs you will — hate, abhor, despise, detest — these are two teams that have it in for each other.

It starts before the first pitch. Like a Greek tragedy, every Yankees-Red Sox game is accompanied by a chorus, although it is not exactly what Euripides had in mind. "Yan-kees Suck!" wafts the echo from the cheap seats at Fenway Park. "Yan-kees Suck!" On a good day the animosity might manifest itself in the form of a Yankees cap plucked from the head of an interloper and ceremoniously placed in a urinal for the masses to defile. On a bad day, it's a hail of batteries aimed at the centerfielder. (Don your batting helmet, Mickey Rivers.) To this day, the Yankees and their fans merit the chilliest New England welcome since the Boston Tea Party.

Of course, it's the other side of the coin when the Red Sox visit Yankee Stadium. Change the noun, keep the verb, chant the chant. "Bos-ton Sucks" bellow the bleacher bums — followed perhaps by a fight in the stands. Or an even nastier chant, one that fully reflects the difference between the two team's fortunes. "Nineteen-Eight-een ... Nine-teen Eight-een" — a reference to Boston's

last World Series championship. When these teams meet, it's a holy war, a jihad. No prisoners will be taken, and neutrality is not allowed. As those Hatfields or McCoys might say: Either you're wit' us or a'gin' us.

The rivalry only begins — or perhaps ends — with baseball. Boston versus New York. It's the Old North Church versus the Statue of Liberty. The Museum of Fine Arts versus the Metropolitan Museum. Baked beans versus hot pastrami. Aerosmith versus the Ramones. The Boston Strangler versus Son of Sam. Nothing is sacred; nothing is off limits.

Recent battles between the clubs have been memorable — the classic 1949 pennant race, the nail-biting 1978 playoff game, the 1999 American League Championship Series — but Red Sox-Yankees hostilities date back almost to the teams' beginnings.

Prior to the 1904 season, the rivalry developed as a result of league president Ban Johnson's forced transfer of some of Boston's best players to New York in order to 'level the playing field.' Johnson's shuffling created ill will in Boston, and it certainly wasn't alleviated when the two teams battled neck-and-neck for the pennant in 1904. The New York club, then known as the Highlanders, and the Boston club, then the Pilgrims and later the Red Sox, met in a season-ending series. Boston fans must have taken a considerable measure of satisfaction as the Pilgrims nosed

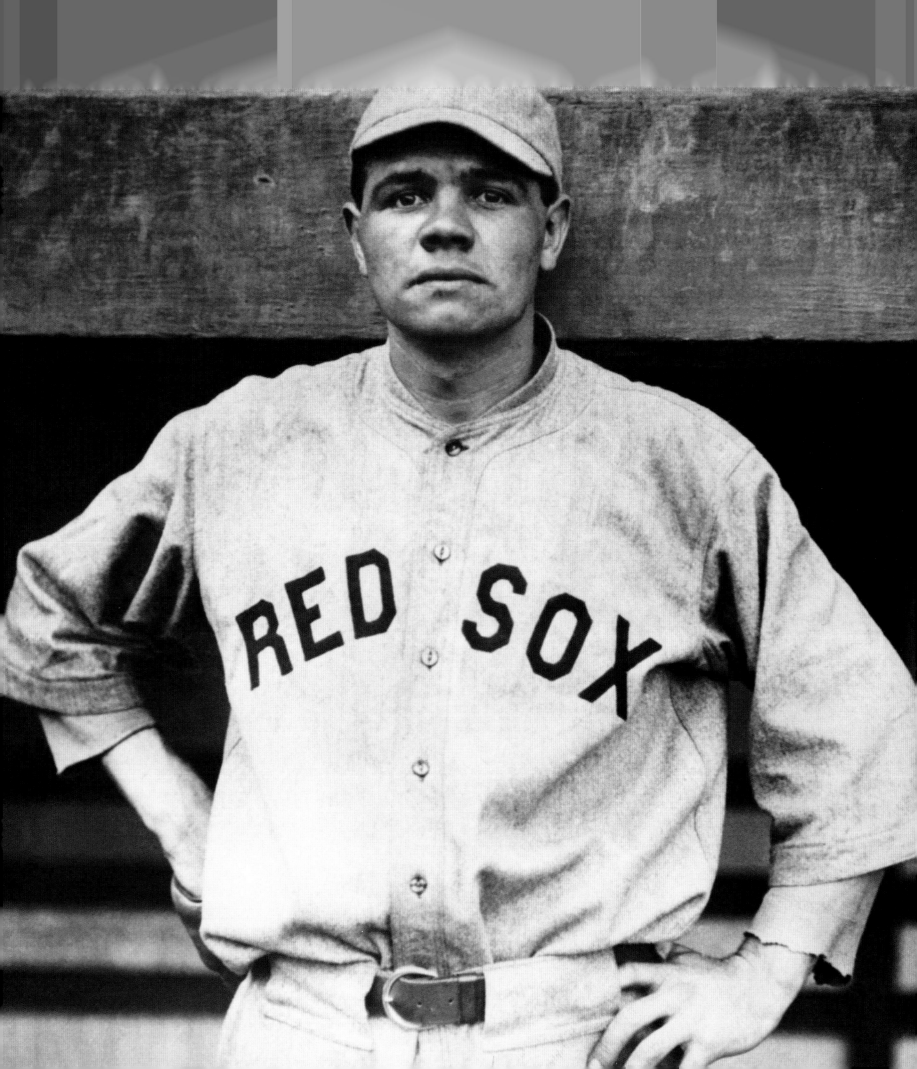

ECHO OF THE
BAMBINO

How does a Red Sox fan define adding insult to injury? Flip through the team's record book and you find the name George Herman "Babe" Ruth all over it — as a pitcher. Although he pitched only five full seasons in Boston, the portly portsider is 15th in career wins with 89, ahead of Dennis Eckersley. Ruth is tied for 10th in career shutouts with 17, ahead of Lefty Grove. He's eighth in complete games (105), ahead of Roger Clemens. He's fourth in career ERA (2.19) just a tick behind Smoky Joe Wood. And he's second in winning percentage (.659), ahead of Cy Young.

Interestingly, Ruth's name doesn't appear among the Red Sox's season or career hitting leaders. One name from the deep, dark past does: Harry Hooper, a Hall of Fame outfielder, a key player on four Red Sox world championship teams between 1912 and 1918, who still holds the team's career record for triples with 160. However, Hooper's greatest contribution to baseball was suggesting that Ruth — who in various seasons led the American League in ERA, shutouts, and complete games — move from the mound to the outfield. That move indirectly led to the Bambino moving from Boston to New York, of course.

HITS ALLOWED/9 INNINGS PITCHED

PLAYER	HITS PER 9/IP	INNINGS PITCHED
1) Pedro Martinez	6.45	664.0
2) **Babe Ruth**	**7.06**	1190.1
3) Joe Wood	7.09	1416.0
4) Carl Mays	7.48	1105.0
5) Dutch Leonard	7.50	1361.1

out the Highlanders for the pennant. New York, though, had an answer. The National League champion New York Giants, and their legendary manager John McGraw, in a snoot over the upstart league, refused to play in the World Series, denying the Pilgrims a chance to repeat as world champions. Boston beat Pittsburgh in 1903 in the inaugural World Series.

Red Sox-Yankees hostilities escalated after a New Yorker, Harry Frazee, bought the Red Sox and proceeded to sell off the team's biggest stars, many to the Yankees, to finance his theatrical projects. The ultimate insult for Bostonians was Frazee selling Babe Ruth to the Yankees in 1920, effecting a shift of baseball power from Boston to New York. The Red Sox, who had won five of the first 15 World Series, fell into a sea of mediocrity while the Yankees became the most dominant team in sports.

the first game, but wound up losing twice, 5-4 and 5-3. And there was the cursed day, January 5, 1920, when Red Sox owner Harry Frazee traded a promising lad named Ruth to the Yankees for $100,000 to help finance the production of the play No No Nanette. A Broadway play, no less.

A rivalry demands at least a measure of equality between the combatants, and through the first three-quarters of the 20th century the Yankees and Red Sox largely competed at different levels. Between 1920 and 1970, the Yankees won 29 pennants, and the Sox finished within nine games of a pennant-winning Yankees team only once — the 1949 heartbreaker. In 1967, during Boston's "Impossible Dream" run to the World Series, the Yankees were mired deep in post-dynasty depression, finishing 20 games off the pace.

Babe Ruth poses with Yankees owner Colonel Jacob Ruppert after signing his first contract with the team.

Amid these heightened passions, the rivalry reached full boil in 1978, that classic season when the teams slugged it out toe to toe, shot for shot, Frazier and Ali on a baseball diamond, going the distance. For Red Sox fans, it was a season at once sacred and obscene, uplifting and heartbreaking, unforgettable and a source of collective amnesia. A season that encapsulated in 162 games — make that 163 — what it is to live and die with the Boys of Fenway.

This is not to dismiss the classic 1949 pennant race, when the Ted Williams-led Red Sox arrived at Yankee Stadium on the season's final weekend with a one-game lead with two games to play, and two 20-game winners scheduled to pitch. The Sox took a 4-0 lead in

As the Bicentennial approached, the playing field between the two teams had leveled out. The Baltimore Orioles dynasty was slipping, while the homegrown Red Sox and the hired-gun Yankees each fancied themselves as the AL East's heir apparent. How did hostilities begin? Let's just call it a cultural thing, the natural friction between the haves and the have-nots. The Yankees traditionally were as blue chip as U.S. Steel, so spoiled by success that they would fire a manager for losing a World Series. The Red Sox were loveable losers with a Bohemian streak, their fans reveling not in box scores or standings but in the pastoral beauty of how-you-play-the-game.

New York's Thurman Munson (left) and Boston's George Scott (third, left) hold back Yankees' Bobby Murcer as Red Sox pitcher Ken Brett (center), and plate umpire Merle Anthony restrain Red Sox catcher, Tom Satriano (4), at Fenway Park, September 24, 1969. The fight started after Satriano tagged Murcer out at the plate.

"They were an elitist corporation with a self-promoted public image of cold arrogance that went against my grain," Bill Lee wrote of the Yankees in his autobiography *The Wrong Stuff*. "The Yankees represented the political right in baseball, while the Red Sox were their opposite number. We were composed of the stuff that made this country great. We were like a bunch of modern-day pilgrims."

Ultimately the political becomes personal, and did things ever get personal. "In the 1970s it was bigger than what it is now," says Don Zimmer, who has been on both sides of the rivalry. "Mainly because there was some players that disliked each other, that made it more intense as a rivalry. Not just the fans, but the players themselves. Graig Nettles and Bill Lee didn't get along. Carlton Fisk and Thurman Munson didn't get along — they were always at each other. It was kind of a war between the players."

How much did Munson loathe Fisk? One day he entered the clubhouse and saw a small mention in the team's media notes that he was second in the league in assists among catchers — two behind Fisk. Munson sought out Yankees public relations director Marty Appel and read him the riot act: "What's the idea of showing me up like this?" Munson roared. "Do you think for one minute he has a better arm than me?" That night Munson dropped not one, not two, but three third strikes. By making the easy pegs to first base for outs, he registered three assists and went ahead of Fisk.

While it's hard to place a date on the commencement of hostilities, the first skirmish dates to mid-1973. After a collision at home plate, Fisk and Munson came up swinging. Michael had missed a squeeze bunt attempt and Fisk tagged out Munson at the plate.

"That wasn't much of a fight," Lee recalls. "Fisk emerged from it with two scratch marks on his cheek. Michael was

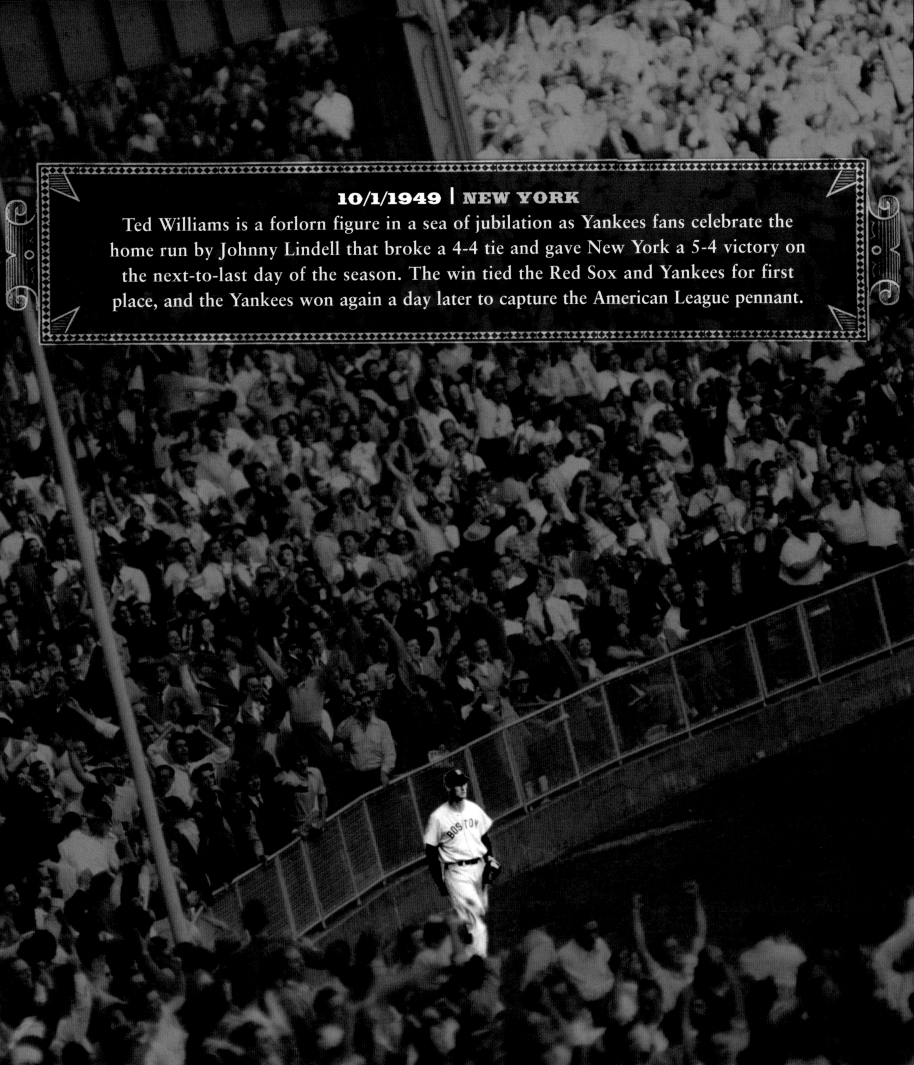

10/1/1949 | NEW YORK

Ted Williams is a forlorn figure in a sea of jubilation as Yankees fans celebrate the home run by Johnny Lindell that broke a 4-4 tie and gave New York a 5-4 victory on the next-to-last day of the season. The win tied the Red Sox and Yankees for first place, and the Yankees won again a day later to capture the American League pennant.

supposed to be feisty, but I never saw him throw an actual punch. The incident may have been forgettable; Lee's rhetoric is not.

Things got ugly on May 20, 1976 at Yankee Stadium, after Lou Piniella tried to take out Fisk at the plate. Fisk objected, and a brawl ensued. Lee, who was the Sox starter, was sucker-punched by Mickey Rivers and body-slammed Gorilla Monsoon-style by Nettles. "I guess Graig's idea of keeping the peace was to arrange for me to get a lot of bed rest in a quiet hospital," Lee said. When the injured Lee showered obscenities at Nettles, all hell broke loose again. "The entire scene became a Fellini movie," Lee recalled. "45,000 Yankees fans are screaming for the lions to devour the Christians." One fan ran on the field and attacked the injured Lee, who could only use his spikes to defend himself. Lee suffered torn ligaments in his pitching shoulder and never was the same. (Payback? Not exactly. In Lee's first start after recovering from the injury, Nettles tagged him for a home run.)

It all was a prelude to the 1978 season, one that Ron Shelton couldn't have scripted any tighter. Let's step back for a moment and meet our contestants.

Zimmer's Red Sox team was as full of promise as a phone call from Ed McMahon. Jim Rice and Fred Lynn seemed on the fast lane to Cooperstown, where they would reunite with Carl Yastrzemski every Induction Day. Dwight Evans was beginning to show the subtle combination of skills that made him arguably the most underrated player of his day. And for once things didn't turn into a Stephen King novel when the other team came up to the plate. The staff ace was Mike Torrez, who had won 14 games for the Yankees in 1977, plus two more in the World Series. Luis Tiant still was practicing modern dance on the mound, Dennis Eckersley was coming into his own during his first life as a starter, and Lee, firmly entrenched in Zimmer's doghouse — that's what you get for calling your manager names and losing seven straight starts — played clubhouse lawyer from the bullpen.

Their adversaries were one of the most disagreeable and dislikable teams in baseball history. Yankees Manager Billy Martin hated his star slugger, Reggie Jackson. Reggie hated Billy.

JIMMIE FOXX & LOU GEHRIG

Munson hated everyone. The previous summer in Boston, Martin and Jackson almost came to blows after Jackson allowed a ball to drop in front of him in the outfield and Martin replaced him in mid-inning. The Bronx Zoo had invaded Fenway Park.

The Red Sox left the gate in 1978 like Secretariat, sprinting through the first half on a 111-win pace. "Boston won again and is 61 and 28, 14 games in front of us. Forget this season. The rest of the year is just playing out the string," wrote Sparky Lyle in *The Bronx Zoo*.

What happened? The Yankees got healthy, recovering from a series of injuries, and laid-back Bob Lemon replaced the fiery Martin. To the north, the Red Sox fell back to earth. Fisk, Lynn, Butch Hobson and Yastrzemski suffered injuries, and the team faltered. "It's all tied up in history, and that old Yankee fear," wrote Thomas Boswell, a columnist for the Washington Post.

"Zimmer had little choice but to push his delicately balanced power plant until black smoke started pouring from the exhaust. Mythology forced his hand. Only a 20-game lead would suffice." Others put it more bluntly. "Some of these guys are choking," said Red Sox first baseman George Scott, who himself was wearing a 0-for-34 collar.

The details are ugly and, by now, familiar. The Red Sox entered September 6½ games ahead of the Yankees, but they lost six of eight prior to a four-game series with the Yankees in Boston. Martin, who had taken exception to Lee comparing him to Hermann Goering, paid a clubhouse boy to hang a dead mackerel in Lee's Fenway Park locker, along with a lewd suggestion of what he could do with it. It was worse on the field for the Sox — they lost all four games by a combined score of 42-9. ("Keeping score, I had begun to feel like an accountant for a Wall Street brokerage firm in the fall of 1929," wrote Roger Angell, a lifelong Red Sox fan, in the New Yorker.) The sweep came to be known as the Boston Massacre, a metaphor which no doubt set Paul Revere spinning in his grave. After losing two more at Yankee Stadium the following week, the Red Sox not only had squandered their 14-game lead but now were 3½ games in arrears.

Yankees' Reggie Jackson (left) is greeted at home plate after belting a three-run home at Fenway Park during the 1978 season. Greeting Jackson left to right: Thurman Munson, Chris Chambliss, and Mickey Rivers.

But one part Rasputin, one part Rocky Balboa, the Red Sox would not die. They won their last eight games in a row, 12 of their last 14. The Yankees clung to one-game lead until the season's final scheduled day. Toronto Blue Jays outfielder Sam Ewing sneaked into Fenway's scoreboard and put up an 8 for Cleveland, New York's opponent, setting the park abuzz. And improbably, life imitated artifice. The Indians hung a nine-spot on Catfish Hunter, the Fenway scoreboard paid tribute to the Cleveland starter ("Thank you, Rick Waits"), Luis Tiant beat Toronto 5-0 and the one-game lead was down to zero. Both teams were 99-63. First one to 100 wins.

The 163rd game. The one constant about baseball is that there always is tomorrow — except, as Yogi Berra might say, when there is no tomorrow. A one-game playoff for the pennant had happened only once previous in baseball history. And the Red Sox lost that one 8-3 to the Cleveland Indians in 1948. This time the suffering in New England would be more exquisite.

If baseball is a game of inches, it never was more apparent than on that October afternoon. History dwells on the moment that Boston's 2-0 lead evaporated, when Bucky Dent, using a bat borrowed from Mickey Rivers, knocked an oh-so-unlikely, three-run tater over the Green Monster, silencing the Fenway Park faithful. "People were stunned," Dent says. "I could feel that eeriness: 'The black cat's here again.'" Torrez, who gave up the home run, remembers it another way: "Another half-inch in on his hands and I may have broken his bat."

Blame right fielder Piniella, too. In the sixth inning with two on, Lynn laced a liner to right field that looked good for extra bases. Piniella, who never was mistaken for Richie Ashburn, had sensed that pitcher Ron Guidry was tiring. After consulting with Munson, Piniella shaded toward the line and turned a possible triple into an easy out. And in the ninth, he made one of the greatest defensive plays ever that didn't result in an out. Piniella lost Jerry Remy's drive in the late afternoon sun. But instead of panicking, he bluffed, positioning himself as if he were about to make the catch. The ball bounced eight feet front of Piniella.

"He didn't see it," Zimmer says. "Piniella's the one who said that the Good Lord put it in his glove." Piniella's trickery kept

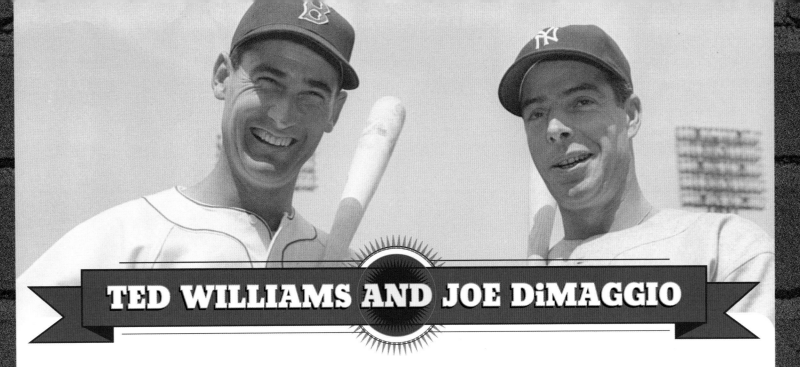

TED WILLIAMS AND JOE DiMAGGIO

The Clipper and The Splinter. Joe D and Teddy Ballgame. The 56-game hitting streak and the .406 season. Hemingway and Updike. For more than a half-century, Joe DiMaggio and Ted Williams have been mentioned in the same breath — even by their teams' owners, who once discussed an even-up swap. Most baseball fans have tended to mention DiMaggio first, ranking him a little higher in the pantheon of baseball immortals. Is this fair? Let's take a look at the numbers.

CAREER NUMBERS

	YRS	G	BA	OBP	SLG	HR	RBI	R	BB	
WILLIAMS	19	2292	.344	.482	.634	521	1839	1798	2019	
DiMAGGIO	13	1736	.325	.398	.579	361	1537	1390	790	

The conclusion? DiMaggio certainly was a great hitter, but Williams arguably was the best ever to slap a pine-tar rag on a piece of ash. Williams has a big lead in virtually every significant offensive category. Pay special attention to his edge in walks, and the corresponding edge in on-base percentage, the most significant hitting statistic. Six times in his career, Williams posted an on-base percentage of .500 or higher, which meant that he reached base more often than he walked back to the dugout. DiMaggio didn't do it once. While both players were injury-prone and missed prime seasons because of military service, Williams had a significantly longer career than DiMaggio did. It is true that Fenway Park was a better hitter's park than Yankee Stadium, and Williams exploited it as well as any hitter ever has — his Beantown average was a stratospheric .361. Performance in road games narrows the gap between the two, but doesn't close it entirely.

CAREER NUMBERS ON THE ROAD

	G	BA	OBP	SLG	HR	RBI	R	
WILLIAMS	1127	.328	.468	.615	273	874	825	
DiMAGGIO	856	.333	.405	.610	213	817	740	

Any edge that fans give to DiMaggio seems built on intangibles. DiMaggio, by all accounts, was one of the great outfielders of all time. But Williams was better than his reputation indicates — his range factor (a measure of chances per game) is better than Lou Brock's and Carl Yastrzemski's. Baserunning? DiMaggio was great, but Williams was at least good. You can't dismiss DiMaggio's collection of championship rings — nine World Series titles in 13 years — but Williams didn't have nearly the supporting cast that DiMaggio did. Plug Williams' bat into the Yankees lineup, and it is reasonable to expect that the team would have had similar success. Unlike DiMaggio, Williams never was married to Marilyn Monroe and Paul Simon never wrote a song about him. But when it came to performing the hardest feat in sports — hitting a baseball — no one did it better than Ted Williams.

BOSTON   NEW YORK
RED SOX   YANKEES

Rick Burleson from reaching third base, where he might have scored and tied the game when Jim Rice flied to the outfield. If Reggie Jackson had been in right field, the extended season might have stretched on into extra innings. But as Yastrzemski observed, "If ifs and buts were candied nuts, we'd all have a helluva Christmas."

That October 2 afternoon was a microcosm of the season. The Red Sox jumped in front and padded their lead. The Yankees fought back, late, strong, and improbably. The wounded Red Sox scratched and clawed, fighting back and falling short by the most miniscule of margins. A single run decided a season: Yankees 5, Red Sox 4.

Boswell dubbed it "The Greatest Game Ever Played"; needless to say, he is not a Red Sox fan. "For once baseball had achieved a moment of genuine dramatic art, a situation that needed no resolution to be perfect," he wrote. "A game, a season, and an entire athletic heritage for two cities had been brought to a razor's edge." Emily Vermeule, a Harvard classics professor writing in the Boston Globe, tried to secure the rhetorical high road. "The Red Sox did not fail, they became immortal," she wrote. "They were worthy of the Sophoclean stage, actors in the traditional and poignant myth, in the long conflict between the larger-than-life hero and inexorable time, native brilliance and predestined ruin, the flukiness of luck, tyche, set against the hardest striving of the individual. It was life in the miniature and not so small at that." Angell was less philosophical as he mused on the moment that Yaz's popup settled into Nettles' glove for the final out: "I think God was shelling a peanut."

Of course, the memories live on. At his baseball camp, Dent constructed his own Little Fenway, with a scoreboard frozen forever

Yankees first baseman Tino Martinez dives into the crowd to make a catch on a foul ball by Red Sox catcher Jason Varitek during the third inning of Game 1 of the ALCS at Yankee Stadium, October 13, 1999.

at 3-2. "The façade is bound to inspire violent flashbacks if you are a Red Sox fan," wrote Dan Shaughnessy in "The Curse of the Bambino." When Zimmer joined the Yankees in 1983 as a coach, whose house did he rent? Dent's. "Everywhere in this place, on every wall, was all this memorabilia, all of it different pictures of that damn home run," Zimmer says. "I turned every one of them around and left them that way for the rest of my stay there."

The Yankees-Red Sox rivalry moved on. Wade Boggs and Don Mattingly battled for the batting title to the last day of the 1986 season. Some dumb kid in the Bronx orchestrated his own little miracle by running onto the field as Mike Stanley was making the final out of a 1993 pennant-race game. The umpire called time, Stanley survived and the Yanks won the game. Pedro schooled Roger. Nomar outslugged Derek. The Yanks had to retreat into the dugout at Fenway during the 1999 playoffs. And the chants echo on.

As do the spirits of the combatants. In the spring of 2001, Bill Lee dredged up the 1978 pennant race like a grave robber,

claiming in a radio interview that Zimmer, who is a close friend of George Steinbrenner, tanked the season. "The fix was in; it had to be," Lee taunted. "How could we cough up that big a lead? Only the Phillies and the Arabs lost in as quick a time."

Sure, Lee's notion is preposterous, even borderline delusional. (Zimmer's sin? He yanked Lee, who had lost seven straight starts in July and August, out of the rotation.) What's the next line of inquiry? Dent's bat was corked? (The Senate Judiciary Committee calls John Milton "Mickey" Rivers.) Was Torrez a double agent, too? (Follow the money.) And why was Piniella on the grassy knoll? (Did he really act alone?) But by its very existence, a conspiracy theory sends one message: It ain't over. The fact that a baseball game can inspire this level of paranoia, almost a quarter century later, speaks volumes about these two teams, that wonderful, awful season, and the fated afternoon that decided it. In the end, the take-home lesson of the summer of 1978 is that to be Red Sox fan is to understand that some sores just don't heal.

THROW IT HERE KNOBBY!

The Title Years

THE RED SOX TEAMS OF 1903-1918

RED SOX TEAMS OF 1903-1918

"Boston clubs have never lost in a World Series and the championship deserves to remain here until the war is won."

RED SOX OWNER HARRY FRAZEE, 1918

Second baseman Dave Shean fielded a grounder and threw to Stuffy McInnis for the final out of the 1918 World Series. McInnis held the ball high and led a charge of Boston Red Sox players for the clubhouse. A brass band played "Tessie," a show tune that had become a Boston ballpark anthem. The Royal Rooters, an always-oiled and boisterous cheering throng of about 300, intercepted the players in front of the dugout and shook hands with their heroes.

It was September 11, 1918, 12 days after Ted Williams was born. The Red Sox were second in headlines to World War I, but second in baseball to none. Boston's superior pitching and defense — a lethal combination in baseball's "dead ball" era — had smothered the Chicago Cubs and delivered the franchise its third World Series title in four years. The Red Sox had won five of the first 15 World Series, two more than any other team.

The Red Sox of the early 1900s were a sparkling jewel on the bedazzling crown that was Boston, the cultural seat of the United States. By the mid-19th century, Boston's 60,000 residents included Daniel Webster and Ralph Waldo Emerson, Horace Mann and Henry Wadsworth Longfellow, Nathaniel Hawthorne and Oliver Wendell Holmes. "All I claim for Boston," Holmes said, "is that it is the thinking center of the continent, and therefore, of the planet." Boston was "The Hub," short for "The Hub of the Universe." Others called Boston the "new Athens," a worthy successor to the birth home of philosophy and science and the nurturer of mathematics and literature.

Exquisite architecture was commonplace in Boston. The Customs House, Faneuil Hall Marketplace, Hotel Vendome and Back Bay's Trinity Church graced the growing city, not to mention scores of elegant homes and mansions. Even New York newspapers urged its readers to "Hurry on!" and see the Bunker Hill Monument, already a world-famous shrine.

The Huntington Avenue Grounds was not among Boston's architectural achievements. The single-level, wooden structure served as the home of Boston's American League team (initially the Somersets, then the Pilgrims and finally the Red Sox) from 1901 to 1911 until Fenway Park was opened in 1912. The expansive and odd-shaped Huntington Avenue Grounds (440 feet to the left-field fence, 635 to center, 290 to right) was built on a wasteland of weeds and lumpy soil near the New Haven and Hartford Railroad tracks and had seats for 9,000.

Most patrons arrived at the ballpark on trolleys or trains. At the first World Series, in 1903, men — and very few women, noted the Boston Globe — filed into the Huntington Avenue Grounds wearing dark suits and bowler hats. The cheapest ticket cost 50 cents. Once the seats were filled, fans were placed beyond the outfielders, swelling attendance to about 11,500 for each of the first three games.

Boston's teams in the early 1900s included the likes of Tris Speaker, Duffy Lewis and Harry Hooper, all great hitters. But when summer turned to autumn, the Red Sox usually won because of the pitching of Cy Young, Bill Dinneen, Smoky Joe Wood, Ernie Shore, Dutch Leonard, Rube Foster and Carl Mays.

> ## "Boston commands special attention as the town which was appointed by the destiny of nations to lead the civilization of North America."
>
> RALPH WALDO EMERSON

And then there was George Herman Ruth, the Babe, who excelled both in the batter's box and on the mound. The Red Sox ranked first or second in the American League in team ERA nine times between 1903 and 1918. In 31 World Series games during that era, they won 13 games by one run and their opponents scored two runs or fewer in 17 games.

Players of that era often were at odds with team ownership and management over money. The players wanted to eliminate the reserve clause in their contracts that bound them to a club until the club disposed of them, a practice that limited a player's negotiating power. World Series financial shares often exceeded a

player's annual income, which is why the Series games were so hotly contested.

The World Series quickly became the country's biggest sporting event. Newspapers covered the spectacle with painstaking thoroughness. The coverage largely was polite. "The best of order prevailed and both teams received liberal applause for good work," reported the Boston Globe after six errors were committed in the first World Series game, October 1, 1903.

The Red Sox won the first World Series and added four more titles in the succeeding 15 years. On the following pages is a look at each of Boston's championship years.

1903 WORLD SERIES

Boston Pilgrims vs. Pittsburgh Pirates

Crowd control was an issue in Boston at the first World Series. Many fans climbed over the wooden fence at the Huntington Avenue Grounds when the police weren't looking, swelling attendance considerably beyond the listed capacity of 9,000. To accommodate everyone, officials allowed fans to stand on the field in foul territory and behind the outfielders.

The overflow crowds had a greater impact on the 1903 Series than any Series since. A ball hit into the crowd in Boston behind the outfielders was a ground-rule double. Reported the Boston Globe after Pittsburgh won the third game: "Four of the five two-base hits made by Pittsburgh were on weak flies into the crowd that the Boston outfielders could have taken behind their backs."

Boston fans displayed great exuberance for the Pilgrims — the team was renamed the Red Sox in 1907 — and none were more boisterous than the Royal Rooters, a raucous group fueled by drink and a passion for the home team. The ringleader of the Rooters was 'Nuf Ced

McGreevey, who got his nickname by ending lengthy disputes with a terse and final "'Nuf Ced." ("Freddy Parent is playing better shortstop than Honus Wagner in this Series. 'Nuf Ced.") The Rooters often broke into their rendition of the show tune "Tessie." When the great Honus Wagner of the Pirates fell into a slump during the Series, the Rooters chided him by changing the song's lyrics from "Tessie, I love you madly" to "Honus, why do you hit so badly?"

The Series was tied after six games. Game 7 was scheduled on a Friday in Pittsburgh, only to be postponed by Pirates owner Barney Dreyfuss, who cited cold weather. Dreyfuss' real motive was getting a bigger gate on Saturday and affording an extra day's rest for pitcher Deacon Phillippe, who had been working more frequently than normal.

The Saturday crowd at Exposition Park was 17,038, far more than there were seats; the overflow was directed to a roped-off area behind the outfielders. Of Boston's 11 hits off Phillippe, five were ground-rule triples into the crowd, several of which could have been caught easily on an unobstructed field. Boston won, 7-3, with Cy

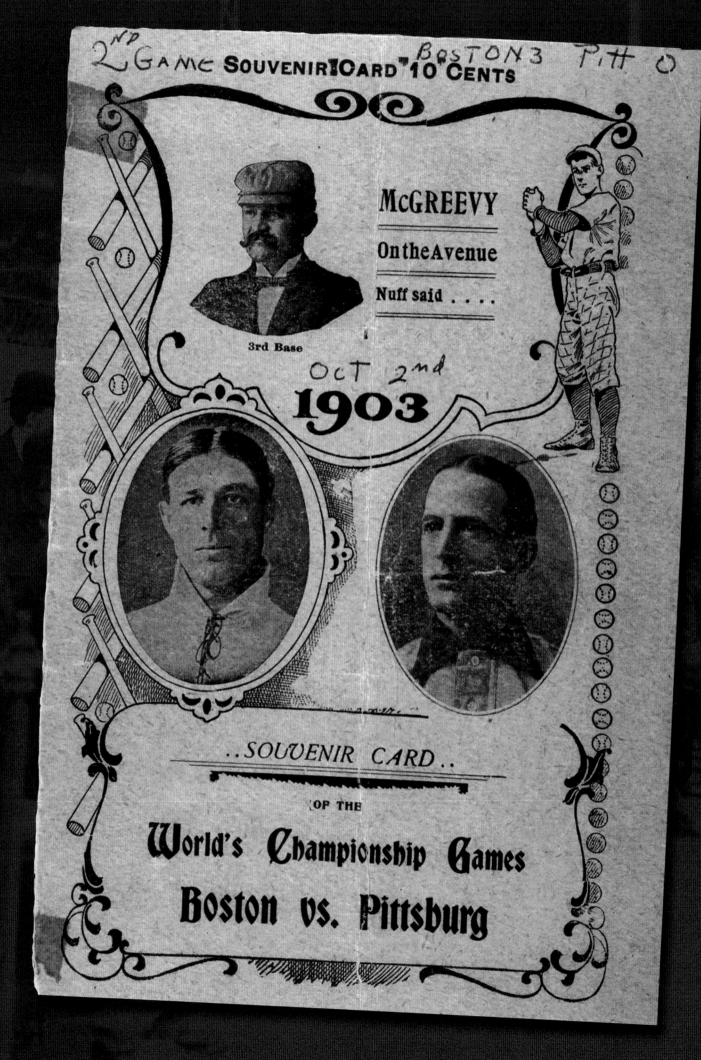

2ND GAME SOUVENIR CARD 10 CENTS BOSTON 3 PITT 0

McGREEVY

On the Avenue

Nuff said . . . .

3rd Base

OCT 2nd

1903

..SOUVENIR CARD..

OF THE

World's Championship Games
Boston vs. Pittsburg

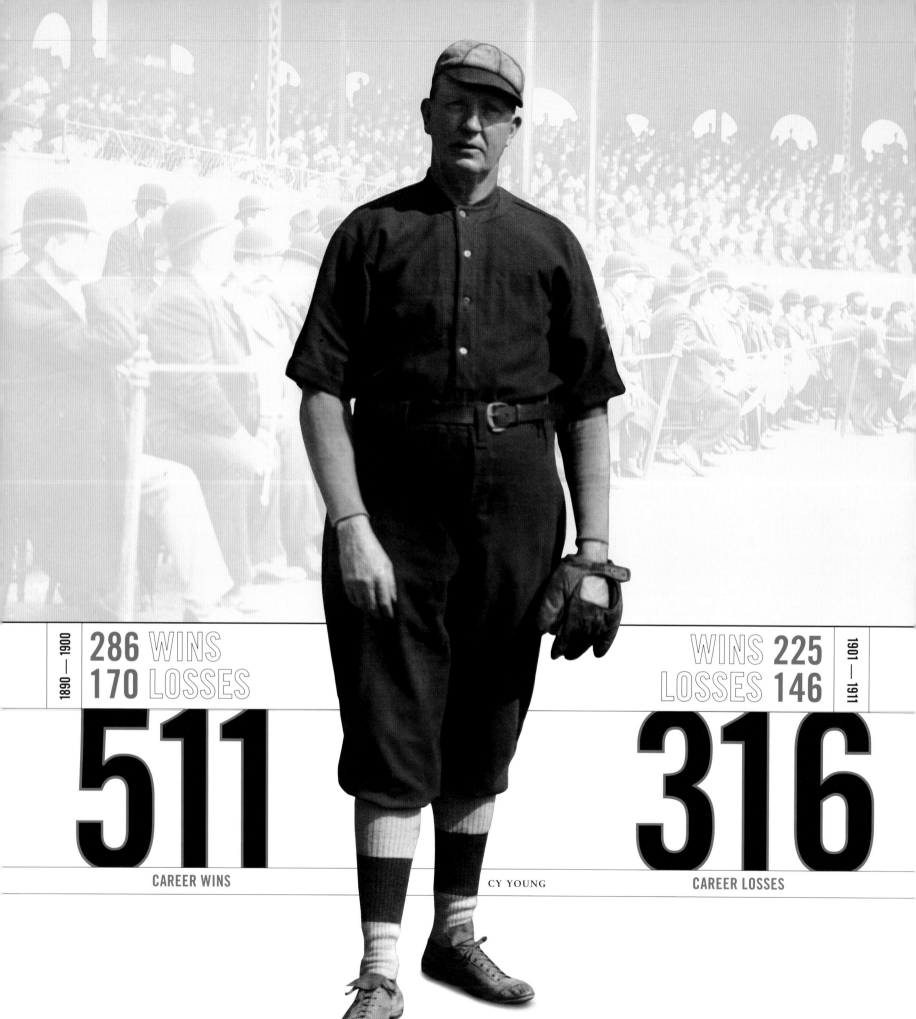

1890—1900

286 WINS
170 LOSSES

511

CAREER WINS

CY YOUNG

WINS **225**
LOSSES **146**

1901—1911

316

CAREER LOSSES

Young on the mound. The Pilgrims then won the Series at home, 3-0, on Bill Dinneen's second shutout and third victory of the Series. Pittsburgh lost the final four games by a score of 31-8.

Boston players earned Series winner shares of $1,182 — less than the Pirates, who received shares of $1,316, thanks to Dreyfuss according his share of $6,669.56 to his players.

The Red Sox won the American League pennant again in 1904, but there was no World Series because the National League champion New York Giants refused to play. Giants owner John Brush and manager John McGraw had nothing but contempt for the upstart American League and its players who had defected from the National League.

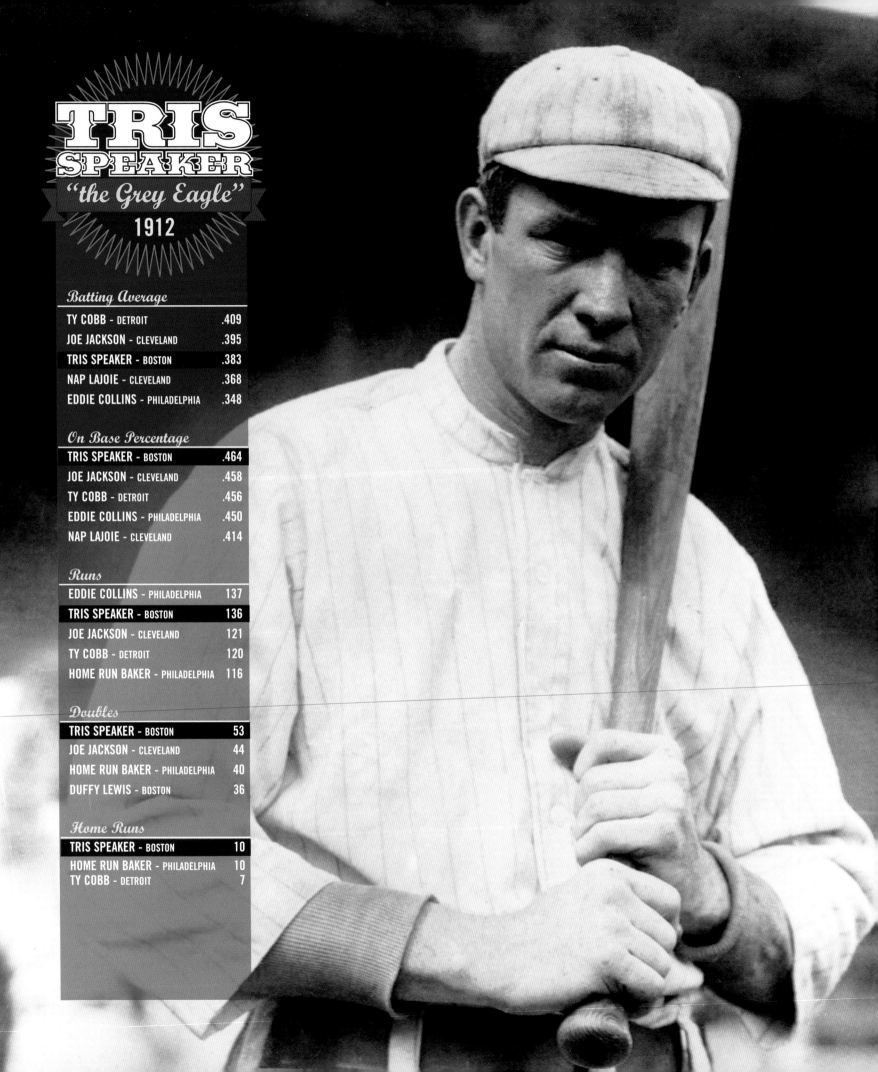

TRIS SPEAKER
"the Grey Eagle"
1912

Batting Average

TY COBB - DETROIT	.409
JOE JACKSON - CLEVELAND	.395
TRIS SPEAKER - BOSTON	.383
NAP LAJOIE - CLEVELAND	.368
EDDIE COLLINS - PHILADELPHIA	.348

On Base Percentage

TRIS SPEAKER - BOSTON	.464
JOE JACKSON - CLEVELAND	.458
TY COBB - DETROIT	.456
EDDIE COLLINS - PHILADELPHIA	.450
NAP LAJOIE - CLEVELAND	.414

Runs

EDDIE COLLINS - PHILADELPHIA	137
TRIS SPEAKER - BOSTON	136
JOE JACKSON - CLEVELAND	121
TY COBB - DETROIT	120
HOME RUN BAKER - PHILADELPHIA	116

Doubles

TRIS SPEAKER - BOSTON	53
JOE JACKSON - CLEVELAND	44
HOME RUN BAKER - PHILADELPHIA	40
DUFFY LEWIS - BOSTON	36

Home Runs

TRIS SPEAKER - BOSTON	10
HOME RUN BAKER - PHILADELPHIA	10
TY COBB - DETROIT	7

1912 WORLD SERIES

Boston Red Sox vs. New York Giants

The World Series was gaining the momentum of an avalanche by 1912. In New York, more than 10,000 jockeyed two hours before game time for prime position to read the play-by-play flashed on an enormous electronic board on the façade of the Times Building in the south end of Times Square. President Taft listened to the Series via Navy wireless on his yacht off Newport. Rhode Island. (The wireless reports and Times Square electronic board reports were communications milestones.) Boston mayor John Fitzgerald, better known as "Honey Fitz," led a pilgrimage to New York, joining hundreds of Royal Rooters on four special trains. Upon arriving, the robust group marched from Grand Central Station up Broadway in a torchlight parade, with Fitzgerald exercising his tenor voice every few blocks. Giants manager John McGraw agreed to write a daily column during the Series for the New York Times. Scalpers sold tickets for $40 to $60 each, more than double what they fetched in the previous Series.

The Red Sox won 105 games in 1912. Their fortunes rode on the right arm of Smoky Joe Wood, who had a 34-5 record. Asked that year if he threw harder than Wood, Walter Johnson replied, "Mister, there's no man alive can throw harder than Joe Wood." The Giants finished with a 103-48 record, three .300 hitters and two 20-game winners, and they stole 319 bases, 67 more than any other team.

The Series hardly was an artistic success; the teams combined for 31 errors. It largely is remembered because the outcome turned on two balls that were not caught in the last half-inning of the final game.

The Series was tied at three games each when Wood took the mound in the seventh inning against Christy Mathewson in Fenway Park. The Giants broke a 1-1 tie in the 10th inning on hits by Fred Merkle and Red Murray. Mathewson needed only three outs, but he didn't get them. Clyde Engle lofted a fly ball to center field that hit Fred Snodgrass' glove and bounded away, enabling Engle to reach second base. After Snodgrass made an over-the-shoulder grab of Harry Hooper's drive, Mathewson walked weak-hitting Steve Yerkes. Tris Speaker lifted a foul pop between home and first base that clearly was first

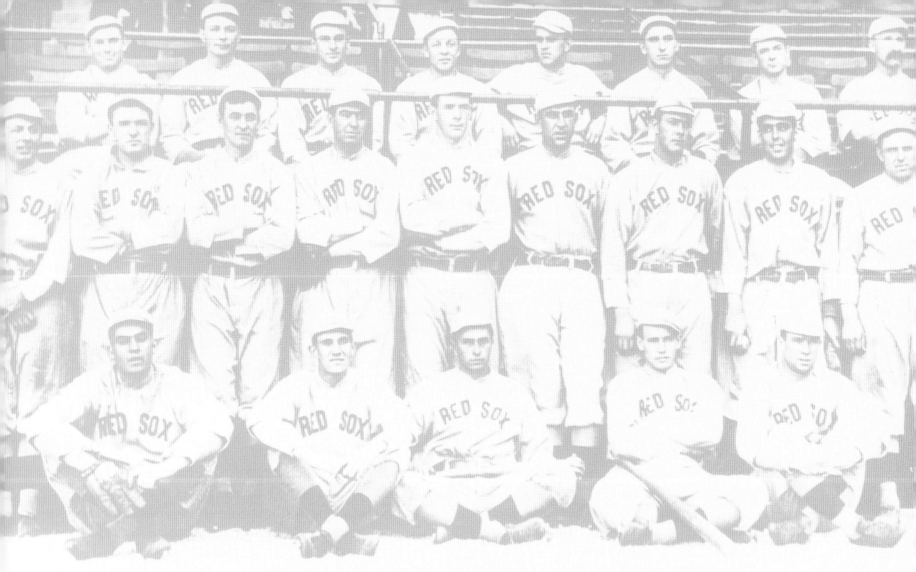

THE BOSTON RED SOX 1912

baseman Merkle's play, but he pulled up when Mathewson called for catcher Chief Myers to catch it. Myers lunged and missed, extending the at-bat for Speaker, who laced a single that scored Engle and moved Yerkes to third. Duffy Lewis, batting .156 in the Series, was walked intentionally. Larry Gardner followed with a sacrifice fly that gave the Red Sox a 3-2 victory.

Boston players each drew a Series share of $4,024, greater than most of their salaries. Snodgrass' error became a part of baseball infamy. He became a wealthy banker and the mayor of Oxnard, California, but when he died in 1974 the headline on his obituary in the *New York Times* read: "Fred Snodgrass, 86, Dead, Ballplayer Muffed 1912 Fly".

FRED SNODGRASS - NEW YORK GIANTS

"For over half a century, I've had to live with the fact that I dropped a ball in the World Series"

CHAMPIONS 1912

RED SOX

WORLD'S SERIES

FENWAY PARK · BOSTON ·

Souvenir Biography and Score Book.

Price, 10 Cents

The Giants-Red Sox battle
was the best World Series to date.

It was not an artistic success; the teams combined for

31 errors.

It largely is remembered because the outcome turned on two balls
that were not caught in the last half-inning of the final game.

WORLD SERIES

Back-to-Back Championship Seasons

1915
BOSTON OVER PHILADELPHIA
in best-of-seven series, 4-1

1916
BOSTON OVER BROOKLYN
in best-of-seven series, 4-1

The Red Sox made short order of the Phillies, who had won only 90 games during the season. Although Fenway Park was just four years old, the Red Sox borrowed new Braves Field for their Series games from their National League brethren because it had a larger capacity than Fenway. Boston crowds of 42,300 and 41,096 generated more revenue for the players to divide, plus the distance from home plate to the left-field fence, 396 feet, helped contain the Phillies' power hitters.

Phillies outfielder Gavvy Cravath was the 1912 major-league leader in home runs with 24, more than four other National League teams and 10 more than the Red Sox's total. Cravath benefited from the Phillies home park, the Baker Bowl, where the right center-field fence was 300 feet from home plate and the right-field fence was 272 feet away.

Rube Foster, Dutch Leonard and Ernie Shore pitched all 44 innings of the Series for Boston and limited the Phillies to 10 runs, a .182 batting average and one home run. The Red Sox didn't need their 20-year-old rookie lefthander, Babe Ruth, who had an 18-8 record during the season. Grover Cleveland Alexander, who would win 372 games during his career, pitched the Phillies to their only victory.

DUTCH LEONARD

The 1916 season started ominously for the Red Sox. They traded star centerfielder Tris Speaker to Cleveland for $50,000 on Opening Day after he resisted a cut in pay to $8,000. Boston had given Speaker an $18,000 salary two years earlier to keep him from jumping to the Federal League, which by 1916 had collapsed.

The Red Sox forged a 91-63 record on the arms of their top five pitchers, who combined for 89 wins. Rube Foster, Dutch Leonard and Ernie Shore, who had been the core of the staff, now had considerable help from Babe Ruth (23-12) and Carl Mays (19-13). The Boston pitchers held Brooklyn to a .200 average and eight runs in the final 40 innings of the Series. In Game 2, Ruth gave up an inside-the-park homer (actually a single that took a bad hop over center fielder Tilly Walker's head) then shut out Brooklyn for 13 innings as Boston won 2-1. Ruth's scoreless-innings streak in Series play would reach 29⅔ innings, a record at the time.

Red Sox infielder Jack Barry probably was the most fortunate player in baseball at the time. He had been on three of Connie Mack's Philadelphia Athletics teams that won the World Series. When Mack began a youth movement in the 1915 season and sold off most of his veteran players, Barry landed with the Red Sox and collected Series winner shares in 1915 and 1916.

Although he never was a regular and never hit higher than .262, Barry earned significant additional income five times in a seven-year span.

Souvenir

SCORE BOOK

Price Ten Cents

RED SOX vs BROOKLYN

AMERICAN LEAGUE · NATIONAL LEAGUE

Jos. J. Lannin Pres.
Boston Red Sox.

Wm. F. Carrigan
Mgr. Boston Red Sox.

Wilbert Robinson
Mgr. Brooklyn Nationals

Charles H. Ebbets
Brooklyn Nationals

1916

WORLD'S SERIES

BRAVES FIELD · BOSTON, MASS.

LINCOLN ENG CO.

RUBE FOSTER
THE RED SOX ACES OF 1915

SEASON **19-8** RECORD

ERNIE SHORE
THE RED SOX ACES OF 1915

SEASON **19-8** RECORD

BABE RUTH

THE RED SOX ACES OF 1915

SEASON **18-8** RECORD

DUTCH LEONARD

THE RED SOX ACES OF 1915

SEASON **15-7** RECORD

1918
WORLD SERIES
Boston Red Sox vs. Chicago Cubs

Interest in baseball waned considerably in 1918. World War I was being waged in Europe, and several harsh winters had depleted the United States' coal supplies. Wheatless Mondays and Wednesdays and meatless Tuesdays were introduced by the U.S. government to help support U.S. troops abroad, and a conservation campaign of "heatless days," "lightless nights" and "gasless Sundays" was launched. Ballpark crowds fell by 17 percent in 1917 and another 41 percent in 1918. Over three years, major-league baseball attendance declined from 6.5 million to 3 million.

In May 1918 the provost marshal of the armed forces, General Enoch Crowder, announced a "work or fight" order, meant to force all men of draft age out of nonessential work and into the military or war-related work. When the war ended in November 1918, 247 major league players were serving in the military; three had been killed in action. The Red Sox played most of the 1918 season with only Harry Hooper and Everett Scott left from their everyday lineup of 1917. With a shortage of players, manager Ed Barrow made a bold move: Babe Ruth would play in the outfield or at first base on the days he didn't pitch.

The Red Sox, who won the American League pennant despite only 75 victories (the season was shortened by one month due to the war), were underdogs in the World Series. The Cubs had the top three winners in the National League: Hippo Vaughn (22), Claude Hendrix (20) and Lefty Tyler (19). Cubs manager Fred Mitchell used only lefthanders Vaughn and Tyler as starters in the Series because it was Boston's practice to deploy the lefthanded-hitting Ruth only against right-handed pitching.

Mitchell's strategy worked. Keeping Ruth on the bench helped the Cubs forge a 1.04 ERA, a Series record. Chicago yielded only six earned runs in six games, but the Cubs were undone by three unearned runs. Boston's victories were by scores of 1-0, 2-1, 3-2 and 2-1. The Red Sox scored just nine runs and batted only .186. Neither team hit a home run, the only homer-less Series ever.

The start of Game 5 was delayed for more than an hour while the players sought a guarantee that they would be paid shares of $2,000 (winning side) and $1,400 (losing side), per an earlier agreement. However, the agreement was based on gate receipts of $150,000 through four

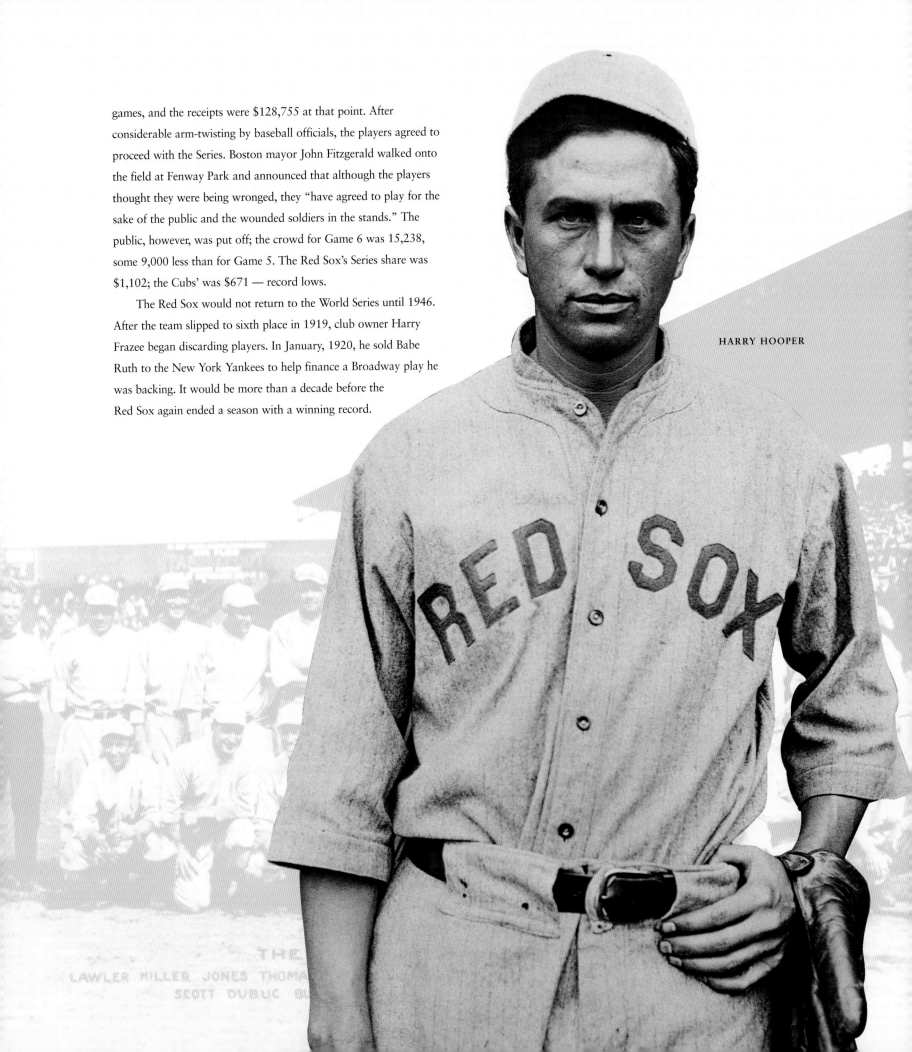

games, and the receipts were $128,755 at that point. After considerable arm-twisting by baseball officials, the players agreed to proceed with the Series. Boston mayor John Fitzgerald walked onto the field at Fenway Park and announced that although the players thought they were being wronged, they "have agreed to play for the sake of the public and the wounded soldiers in the stands." The public, however, was put off; the crowd for Game 6 was 15,238, some 9,000 less than for Game 5. The Red Sox's Series share was $1,102; the Cubs' was $671 — record lows.

The Red Sox would not return to the World Series until 1946. After the team slipped to sixth place in 1919, club owner Harry Frazee began discarding players. In January, 1920, he sold Babe Ruth to the New York Yankees to help finance a Broadway play he was backing. It would be more than a decade before the Red Sox again ended a season with a winning record.

HARRY HOOPER

The Unforgettables

TED'S 1941 SEASON-ENDING DOUBLEHEADER

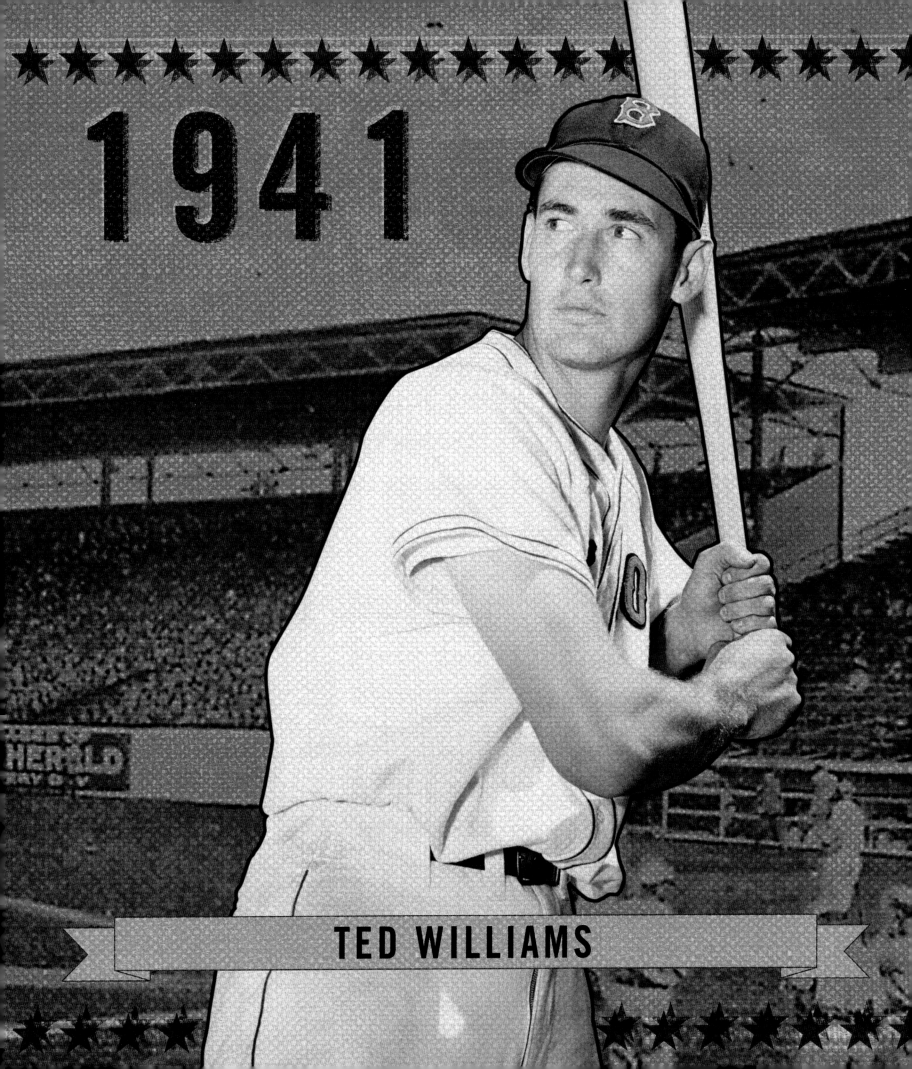

1941

TED WILLIAMS

TED'S 1941 SEASON-ENDING DOUBLEHEADER

It is undoubtedly the most famous downtown stroll in baseball history, a lazy, weekend ramble whose destination was nowhere and everywhere. While Ted Williams carried no bags as he wandered the streets of Philadelphia on that September Saturday night in 1941, the walk must have been exhausting. He was, after all, carrying the weight of the world on his slender shoulders.

Williams was just 23 years old. The Kid really was a kid. Yet he was kneeling in the on-deck circle of baseball history. With two games remaining in the 1941 season — a Sunday afternoon doubleheader with the Philadelphia Athletics at Shibe Park — Williams had in his sights the specter of being the game's first .400 hitter since the New York Giants' Bill Terry hit .401 in 1930.

The story goes that the night before the doubleheader, after going 1 for 4 in that day's game to drop his average to .39955, Williams toured downtown Philadelphia with Red Sox clubhouse attendant Johnny Orlando — and did a lot of thinking about this .400 business while on the extended walk. The story continues that Orlando popped into a bar or two along the way, and that Williams, ever the all-American boy, tossed down a couple of malteds.

The next day, Teddy Ballgame belted shots all over Shibe Park, amassing six hits in eight at-bats in the doubleheader. When the day and the season and the quest were over, Williams was the owner of a .406 batting average. As sports writer Jack Malaney put it so well in the next day's Boston Post: "All hail Thumping Theodore Samuel Williams, the greatest batsman in a decade and one of the greatest of any time, because of his deeds during the 1941 season."

Deeds … indeed. But if Williams really knew how big a deal the season-ending doubleheader with the Athletics was going to be,

chances are he might have reached for something a tad more stiff than a malted. Pressure? What Williams did not know, couldn't possibly have known, is that his .406 season would turn out to be a dividing line in baseball history. For in all the seasons that have been logged since 1941, of all the hopeful maybes who have dug in against imposing pitchers, and even more imposing history, and attempted to match or eclipse Williams, nobody has come close.

When Rod Carew flirted with .400 in 1977, it was such a big deal that it made the cover of *Time* magazine. Carew settled in at an impressive, but not historic, .388. Three years later, George Brett's bid ended at .390. The best Tony Gwynn did was .394 — in the ballpark with Williams, if you will, but an abbreviated quest because of the players' strike that ended the 1994 season. Wade Boggs, the Red Sox's best hitter for average since Williams, once hit .368. A great season, yet without a hint of 1941 to it.

Come next season, the game's top batsmen again will be dreaming — daydreaming, really — of becoming baseball's first .400 hitter in more than six decades. In 1941, Williams was hoping to become baseball's first .400 hitter in a little more than one decade. "The 1941 season really was the end of an era," says Dominic DiMaggio, Williams' Red Sox teammate and kid brother of the great Joe DiMaggio. "It was the last season before World War II. After the war, Jackie Robinson broke the color barrier. And later on we had

What Williams did not know that day, couldn't possibly have known, is that his .406 season would turn out to be a dividing line in baseball history. For in all the seasons that have been logged since 1941, of all the hopeful maybes who have dug in against imposing pitchers, and even more imposing history, and attempted to match or eclipse Williams, nobody has come close.

television, expansion, teams moving, all kinds of things. So you look closely at 1941 and you realize how special it was. It was a fabulous year in all respects, and we didn't even know it at the time."

The dominant baseball story of the 1941 season was Joe DiMaggio's 56-game hitting streak. It was an ever-building, ever-widening story that captured the imagination of millions of Americans — whether they were ball fans or not — and when it ended on July 17, 1941, it was shocking, stop-the-presses news. It didn't hurt DiMaggio any that he was a more glamorous player than Williams, doing business with a more glamorous team, playing in a

town whose top athletes palled around with chorus girls, mobsters and Runyonesque barkeeps. Thus, as the season was winding down and Williams was making his bid for .400, the Story of the Year already had been written and filed: DiMaggio's hitting streak.

When Williams achieved his goal, he didn't have a horde of nationally known sports writers weighing in from Shibe Park; it wasn't even the lead story of the day. Most newspapers seemed more interested in the Joe Louis-Lou Nova heavyweight boxing showdown scheduled for the following night in New York at the Polo Grounds. (To understand the hugeness of a heavyweight title fight in those

The dominant baseball story of the 1941 season was Joe DiMaggio's 56-game hitting streak. It was an ever-building, ever-widening story that captured the imagination of millions of Americans — whether they were ball fans or not — and, when it ended, on July 17, 1941, it was shocking, stop-the-presses news.

days, consider this: a mob of 56,549 fight fans turned out at the Polo Grounds to watch Louis KO Nova in the sixth round. A day earlier in Philadelphia, 10,268 showed up at Shibe Park to watch Williams make history. More than 60 years later, we still are waxing about Ted's .406 batting average, whereas the Louis-Nova fight is an obscure line in boxing almanacs.)

Williams didn't even have the spotlight to himself in the Boston newspapers. The sports editors of the day saved the biggest and boldest headlines for the Boston

College-Tulane football game played in New Orleans that Saturday. Boston's best-known sports columnist of the time, the Daily Record's Dave Egan, a man who later would become Williams' longtime nemesis, managed to take in both the BC-Tulane game in New Orleans and the Louis-Nova fight in New York — but he didn't have room on his itinerary for Ted's quest for .400.

It's not as if the possibility of Williams hitting .400 sneaked up on everybody. The Kid was a smash hit when he broke into the big

leagues in 1939, hitting .327 with 31 home runs and a league-leading 145 RBI. The next season, Williams hit .344. When the 1941 season opened, Williams immediately made his case: He hit an Opening Day home run in Detroit, followed by a home run at Chicago's Comiskey Park that was said to travel some 500 feet. He had arrived late for spring training and been hampered by an ankle injury, but, the season in bloom, the games being played for real, Williams swung with a vengeance. He hit .557 during a 16-game stretch in May, and at one point his average was .438.

EVEN THE GREATEST HITTERS EXIST IN THE SHADOW OF TED WILLIAMS. DESPITE LEADING THE LEAGUE IN WALKS EIGHT TIMES AND MISSING VIRTUALLY FIVE ENTIRE SEASONS TO MILITARY SERVICE, THE "SPLENDID SPLINTER" REMAINS THE MODEL TO

TED WILLIAMS' STRIKE ZONE

WHICH ALL OTHERS ARE COMPARED. THE CHART IS AN ENLARGED VERSION OF WILLIAMS' STRIKE ZONE. THE NUMBER ON EACH BALL REPRESENTS WILLIAMS' LIKELY BATTING AVERAGE IF EVERY PITCH CROSSED THE PLATE AT THAT LOCATION.

When the American League and National League convened for the All-Star Game, Williams was hitting .405 and DiMaggio's hitting streak stood at 48 games. The Red Sox opened the second half of the season in Detroit, and, ominously, Williams suffered another ankle injury. He spent the next two weeks on the bench, mostly watching, occasionally pinch-hitting, and his average dipped to .393.

The Red Sox played their final home game of the 1941 season on Sunday, September 21, after which the team traveled to

Washington and Philadelphia for the final six games of the schedule. Williams was at .406 when the trip began; after getting only two hits in 10 at-bats against the Senators, he was down to .402.

Though the Red Sox were well out of the pennant race by September — they finished in second place, 17 games behind the Yankees — Williams' quest for a .400 season kept the team in the headlines. Things even turned controversial: When Williams was called safe at first in the fourth inning of the September 24 game at Washington, some

something to get his mind off the great quest, for it was clearly an obsession at this point. Pitcher Charlie Wagner, Williams' roommate on the 1941 Red Sox, recalled 60 years later: "Those last few days of the season, it's all he thought about. Ted always got up early in the morning, but that weekend in Philadelphia he was up even earlier than usual. I remember that Saturday morning, the day before the season ended, I was still in bed and I could hear him shaving in the bathroom. He didn't talk much about it, but you knew it was on his mind."

.300	.320	.320	.330	.330	.315	.310
.310	.340	.340	.350	.340	.340	.320
.310	.310	.340	.350	.340	.340	.320
.340	.380	.380	.400	.390	.390	.320
.360	.390	.390	.400	.390	.390	.320
.360	.390	.390	.400	.380	.380	.310
.320	.340	.340	.330	.300	.300	.280
.320	.340	.330	.330	.275	.270	.260
.280	.300	.300	.300	.260	.250	.250
.270	.290	.300	.300	.250	.240	.240
.250	.270	.270	.260	.240	.240	.230

argued that the fix was in. The Boston Herald reported that many of the 7,500 fans at Griffith Stadium "hooted loud and long" when umpire Bill Grieve ruled that Ted had beaten out the grounder.

The Red Sox next traveled to Philadelphia to close the season against Connie Mack's Athletics. Friday was an off-day, and Williams went to Shibe Park with Red Sox coaches Frank Shellenback and Tom Daly and backup infielder Scoops Carey for an afternoon of batting practice. No doubt Williams wanted to get out of his room and do

If Williams feared anything, it was that Mack, the 79-year-old owner/manager of the Athletics, would not allow his pitchers to throw anything "good" to Williams. It was a ploy that Mack often had used against Williams. The logic was simple: Why allow a team's best player to beat you? But the word was that Mack was going to give Williams a sporting chance to hit .400. Bert Whitman wrote in the Saturday, September 27 *Boston Herald*: "We understand the A's pitchers will pitch to him, will dare him to hit their best stuff, properly delivered.

This is the sporting thing to do, and the A's front office realizes that the crowd wants to see Ted hit, and not walk." Al Brancato, a 22-year-old infielder on the 1941 Athletics, recalled a clubhouse meeting before the series in which Mack "... stood right in the middle of the room and made it quite clear to us that we were going to pitch to Ted Williams. He wanted Ted to earn it, which means we weren't going to give him anything to hit, but that we weren't going to walk him, either."

Only about 1,000 fans showed up at Shibe Park that afternoon. Mack's pitching rotation for the series was three rookies, the first a 30-year-old knuckleball artist named Roger Wolff who was making just his second big-league start. (Finding a home with the Washington Senators in 1945, Wolff would win 20 games.) Williams drew a walk his first time up. In his next at-bat, he doubled to right-center to improve his average to .402. In his next two tries, he flied to right and hit a foul pop to first. With two outs in the ninth, he waved at a knuckleball for strike three. He went 1 for 4 in the Red Sox's 5-1 victory, dropping his average to .39955.

There has been a lot of revised, tinkered history over the years claiming that Williams, had he sat out the season-ending doubleheader, still would have had his .400 season, since the .39955 would have been rounded up to .400. Not so. If you don't hit .400, you don't hit .400, and no amount of mathematical wizardry was going to turn .39955 into .400. Wrote Bert Whitman in the September 28 Herald: "If it rains (Sunday) and washes out the last day of the season doubleheader between the Red Sox and A's, a

just 20 years old, and had spent most of the season in the minors. This historic game would be just his fourth major-league appearance, which means Williams didn't know much about him. But the opposing players sure knew about Ted. Wrote Williams in his autobiography, My Turn At Bat:

"As I came to bat for the first time that day, the Philadelphia catcher, Frankie Hayes, said, 'Ted, Mr. Mack told us if we let up on you he'll run us out of baseball. I wish you all the luck in the world, but we're not giving you a damn thing.' Bill McGowan was the plate umpire, and I'll never forget it. Just as I stepped in, he

"There was no way he was going to miss that last day," said Dom DiMaggio. "If anything, there might have been talk he'd sit out the second game if he had enough hits in the first game to hit .400. But he was going to play in that first game." Added Charlie Wagner, "I don't remember him saying anything about not playing. I don't think he ever considered it."

tremendous controversy might start as to whether Ted Williams, the Hub's Splendid Splinter, is entitled to be listed among the immortal .400 hitters in the majors."

"There was no way he was going to miss that last day," Dom DiMaggio said. "If anything, there might have been talk he'd sit out the second game if he had enough hits in the first game to hit .400. But he was going to play in that first game." Added Charlie Wagner, "I don't remember him saying anything about not playing. I don't think he ever considered it."

Starting for Philadelphia in the Sunday opener was righthander Dick Fowler. Unlike the knuckleballing Wolff, this rookie was a kid,

called time and slowly walked around the plate, bent over and began dusting it off. Without looking up, he said, 'To hit .400 a batter has got to be loose. He has got to be loose.' I guess I couldn't have been much looser."

Williams got ahead on the count 2-and-0. Fowler threw a fastball, and Williams lined it to the right of first baseman Bob Johnson for a single. "That's the one I remember the most," Al Brancato said. "Our regular first baseman was Dick Siebert, but he was out and had gone home for the season. Bob Johnson usually played the outfield. That ball that went by him was hit so hard that you kind of knew the way the day was going to go."

And so it went. In his next at-bat Williams hit his 37th home run of the season, a shot that traveled over the right-field wall at Shibe Park and out onto 20th Street. Newspaper accounts estimated the distance at 440 feet.

When Williams came to bat in the sixth inning, lefty Porter Vaughan was pitching. Ted singled. In the seventh inning, facing Vaughan again, he hit a liner over Johnson's head for his fourth hit of the game, raising his average to .405. In his fifth at-bat, in the ninth, he hit a hard grounder to second baseman Crash Davis (yes, that Crash Davis) that was bobbled — an error — and Williams ended the game 4 for 5.

Williams now was hitting .404. He could have sat out the second game and nobody would have been able to wage an argument that his .400 season was tainted. Even if he had gone 0 for 4, his season-ending average would have been .4004376. Williams played — and continued to hit.

Mack's choice to pitch the second game was 22-year-old Fred Caligiuri. A "pretty slick righthander," according to one newspaper account, Caligiuri had spent most of the season with the Wilmington Blue Rocks in the Class B Interstate League, and had been the league's pitcher of the year. His season-ending start for the A's was just his fifth such big-league assignment.

Facing Caligiuri in the second inning, Williams reached on a ground-ball single between first and second. In the fourth inning, he fouled off a 2-and-0 pitch and then hammered a fastball to right-center for a double. "The ball plunked into the loudspeaker horns on the wall, high up, punched a clean hole in one of them, and fell back on the playing field, just a two-bagger ... but a tremendous clout just the same," reported the Boston Herald.

By the time Williams came to bat in the seventh inning, the sky was darkening and sports writers were filing their celebratory prose. Williams flied to left, and his magical season was in the books: .4057. There being no controversy with the math this time, it was rounded off to .406.

Overshadowed by Williams' performance in the second game was the curtain-call performance of Lefty Grove, making his final big-league start. Grove had had his greatest years in Shibe Park, pitching for Mack's Athletics, but now he was sweating out his eighth, and final, season with the Red Sox. The 41-year-old was torched for three runs in the first inning, prompting the Herald's Whitman to refer to him as " ... that pathetic figure." But what praise the knights of the keyboard heaped upon Williams.

"Ted Williams put on one of the most spectacular last-day batting splurges in the history of major-league baseball," wrote an enthusiastic Whitman. Fred Wright of the *Boston Traveler* barely could contain himself: "Ted did it! That, in three words, is a summarization of Boston's major-league baseball for 1941." Gushed the *Boston Globe*: "Four hundred and six, or .4057 if you want to split decimal points. That's the fabulous figure with which Ted Williams finished the American League season today, as he became the first major-league hitter to reach .400 in 11 years ... by unleashing a hat-hoisting garrison finish."

Yet all they knew then was that Williams had become baseball's first .400 hitter since 1930, that he was the first American Leaguer to do it since the Detroit Tigers' Harry Heilmann hit .403 in 1923, that he was the first Boston player to do it since Hughie Duffy's .438 season with the 1894 Beaneaters.

Williams didn't just close out a season when he hit .406, he closed out a distinct chapter in baseball history. More than 60 years later, the game's best and brightest hitters still are trying to recapture the magic of that September Sunday afternoon at Shibe Park.

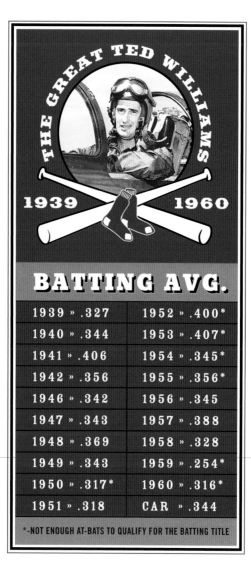

THE GREAT TED WILLIAMS

1939 ☆ 1960

BATTING AVG.

1939 » .327	1952 » .400*
1940 » .344	1953 » .407*
1941 » .406	1954 » .345*
1942 » .356	1955 » .356*
1946 » .342	1956 » .345
1947 » .343	1957 » .388
1948 » .369	1958 » .328
1949 » .343	1959 » .254*
1950 » .317*	1960 » .316*
1951 » .318	CAR » .344

*-NOT ENOUGH AT-BATS TO QUALIFY FOR THE BATTING TITLE

TED'S LAST HOME RUN

SEPTEMBER 28, 1960

THOSE FANS, HOWEVER SPARSE AND BONE-CHILLED, WERE PART OF THE GLORIOUS MOMENT WHEN IN HIS FINAL AT BAT WILLIAMS LAUNCHED A 1-1 PITCH FROM JACK FISHER INTO THE RED SOX BULLPEN. EVEN AS BEDLAM ENSUED AT THE OLD BALLYARD, THE 42-YEAR-OLD WILLIAMS, EVER THE STATESMAN, SHOWED LITTLE EMOTION AS HE QUICKLY CIRCLED THE BASES WITH HIS HEAD DOWN, HUMBLY.

TED'S FINAL AT-BAT

There are exits, there are graceful exits, and then there is the Ted Williams exit, which came on a cool, gray day with Fenway filled only to about a third of capacity. Earlier in the week, Red Sox owner Tom Yawkey had announced that Williams would be retiring, but many in Boston questioned the legitimacy of the retirement. With Baltimore in town for the Sox's final two home games, Williams was honored briefly by Boston mayor John Collins. Teddy Ballgame, after taking one last swipe at the "Knights of the Keyboard" and the "disagreeable things that have been said about me," conceded that "baseball has been the most wonderful thing in my life." He concluded his brief remarks by saying he couldn't think of a better place to spend his 19-year career than Boston, "with the greatest owner in baseball and the greatest fans in America."

Those fans, however sparse and bone-chilled, were part of the glorious moment when in his final at-bat Williams launched a 1-1 pitch from Jack Fisher into the Red Sox bullpen. Even as bedlam ensued at the old ballyard, the 42-year-old Williams, ever the statesman, showed little emotion as he quickly circled the bases with his head down, humbly. The Sox finished the season in New York, but Williams had decided he would end his career in his park. The 521st and final home run of Williams' career came in the House that Ted Built.

1975 WORLD SERIES, GAME 6

OCTOBER 21, 1975

THE VIDEO FROM AN NBC CAMERA IS AS MUCH A PART OF BASEBALL AS BABE, CAL AND THE McGWIRE/SOSA HOME-RUN CHASE. BUT THE STRANGE THING ABOUT CARLTON FISK'S "IF IT STAYS FAIR IT'S GONE" GAME-WINNING HOME RUN IN GAME 6 OF THE 1975 WORLD SERIES, IS THAT IT WAS JUST ONE OF BOSTON'S MIRACLE MOMENTS FROM THE 12-INNING EPIC BATTLE WITH THE CINCINNATI REDS.

DWIGHT EVANS' CATCH

BERNIE CARBO'S HOME RUN

CARLTON FISK'S HOME RUN

After three rain-induced postponements, the game finally began on Tuesday, October 21, at Fenway Park. The Red Sox, who trailed 3-games-to-2 in the series, took an early 3-0 lead. But the Big Red Machine was leading, 6-3, heading into the home half of the eighth inning.

With two on and two outs, Red Sox manager Darrell Johnson called on Bernie Carbo to pinch hit again. (Carbo previously had cracked a pinch-hit homer in the Series.) Carbo barely fouled off a 2-2 pitch from reliever Rawley Eastwick, then sent the next offering into the center field bleachers, and Fenway shook to its core as the Sox tied the score, 6-6.

The score was still tied in the 11th inning, and with a man on base, Cincinnati's Joe Morgan sent a deep shot to right that seemed destined to leave the yard and give the Reds a two-run lead. Just as heads began to hang in disbelief throughout Fenway, Dwight Evans made a spectacular grab to the right of the outfield bullpens, then spun and threw a bullet toward the infield that started an inning-ending double play.

That helped set the stage for Fisk's heroics in the 12th, memorialized by Dick Stockton's oft-heard call of the shot: "He swings, long drive to left field. If it stays fair it's gone … HOME RUN! The Red Sox win and the Series is tied." Without question, Miracle Three of the evening had been accomplished.

34-5*	.872*	38	35*	10*	344	258	1.91
* LEAD THE LEAGUE	W-L	PCT.	GS	CG	SHUTOUTS	IP	SO	ERA

JOE WOOD VS WALTER JOHNSON

SEPTEMBER 6, 1912

WALTER JOHNSON, THE BIG TRAIN, WAS THE LEGENDARY WASHINGTON SENATORS FIREBALLER; SMOKY JOE WOOD WAS THE NEW KID ON THE BLOCK.

SMOKY JOE WOOD

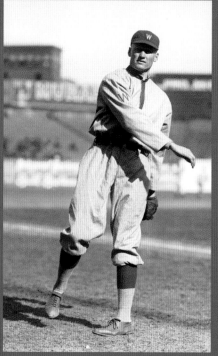

WALTER JOHNSON

I f this match-up had been played out in the modern era of televised sports, it well could have been the most-watched pay-per-view event of all-time. Instead, it was played in 1912, when Fenway Park was brand new. Walter Johnson, the Big Train, was the legendary Washington Senators fireballer; Smoky Joe Wood was the new kid on the block. Earlier that season Johnson won 16 straight games, and Wood was working on a 13-game streak. Baseball's two most dominant pitchers were not scheduled to face each other during the Series, but the Senators boldly challenged the Red Sox to pit Wood against Johnson; Senators manager Clark Griffith went so far as to say Wood would be "a coward" not to face Johnson. The challenge was accepted, and Fenway overflowed with fans for the game. For the first and only time in the history of Fenway Park, fans who didn't have a seat were allowed to stand along both foul lines and behind home plate, forcing the players to come out of the dugout in order to see the duel.

The game lived up to all the hype. Wood beat Johnson, 1-0. The Sox scored the only run with two outs in the sixth when Tris Speaker and Duffy Lewis hit back-to-back doubles. Wood won his 14th straight game by yielding six hits and fanning nine. Johnson gave up five hits and struck out five. Wood went on to win 34 games that season.

1999 ALL-STAR GAME

JULY 13, 1999

WHEN THE GAME STARTED, PEDRO MARTINEZ PITCHED HIMSELF INTO THE ALL-STAR GAME RECORD BOOK BY STRIKING OUT THE FIRST FOUR HITTERS AND FIVE OVERALL. "I THINK IT MAKES IT A LITTLE MORE SPECIAL, BEING HERE IN BOSTON," MARTINEZ SAID AFTER WINNING THE GAME'S MVP AWARD.

TED WILLIAMS WITH TONY GWYNN

If there is a better sports town in America than Boston it better start proving it, because Beantown has held top honors since the days of Russell, Orr and Ted. Even when the teams are losing, the talk is heated and passionate; the support solid and enduring. All that bragging aside, Boston proved it again when the 1999 All-Star Game festivities were played out at Fenway Park. In addition to the normal buzz that alone would surround the event, Major League Baseball wrapped in its All-Century team celebration for good measure. All the planned events seemed to fall short of what it meant to have hometown heroes Martinez and Nomar Garciaparra playing feature roles for the American League. The dramatic entry of living members of the All Century Team set the tone for the impromptu, emotional show of respect at the feet (and golf cart) of

Boston's best ever, Ted Williams, stirred a fever-pitched crowd. Mark McGwire, Sammy Sosa, Tony Gwynn, Ken Griffey, Jr. and other greats of past and present encircled and honored the game's greatest hitter. For pure goosebumps-and-shivers moments, that gathering ranks among baseball's best.

When the game started, Martinez pitched himself into the All-Star Game record book by striking out the first four hitters and five overall. "I think it makes it a little more special, being here in Boston," Martinez said after winning the game's MVP award. "Representing the decade, the last one of the century. Being there with all those players around us, I never, never expected it." Said the 80-year-old Williams: "I can only describe it as great. Hell, I haven't had a base hit in 30 years, and I'm a better hitter now than I've ever been in my life."

PEDRO DEFLATES THE INDIANS

GAME 5 1999 AMERICAN LEAGUE DIVISION SERIES

Boston fandom quickly discovered many things about the magnificent Pedro Martinez. Likewise, Pedro soon became acclimated with that fandom. Beyond knowing about his fastball, changeup and big-game dominance, fans know Pedro doesn't believe in the so-called Curse of the Bambino. "Wake up the damn Bambino and have him face me. Maybe I'll drill him in the ass," Martinez once said. No player in Red Sox history lends more credence and meaning to that statement, especially after Martinez's series-clinching performance in Game 5 of the 1999 American League Division Series at Cleveland's Jacobs Field.

Martinez suffered a pulled back muscle in the opening game of the series, and the

prospects for his return in the playoffs was dim. After the Red Sox lost the first two games by a combined score of 14-3, it appeared as if the Curse had reared its ugly head again. But when word filtered through Boston that Pedro might be available for the fifth game, the scrappy Sox seemed to hear the buzz and responded with wins in Games 3 and 4 by a combined score of 32-10. Martinez did not start Game 5, but he went to the mound in the fourth inning with the score tied, 8-8. Pitching six hitless innings, Martinez gave his battle-weary mates just the lift they needed as they scrounged together four more runs to take the game, 12-8, and the series, 3-games-to-2. His teammates carried him off the field in as emotional a display as has ever been broadcast in the history of televised sports.

CLEMENS' 20 STRIKEOUT GAME

APRIL 29, 1986

ROGER CLEMENS THREW MOST OF HIS 138 PITCHES IN THE MID-90 MPH RANGE; 97 WERE STRIKES AND ONLY 10 WERE PUT IN PLAY. THE SPARSE CROWD OF 13,414 WITNESSED PERHAPS THE MOST DOMINANT PERFORMANCE EVER BY A PITCHER.

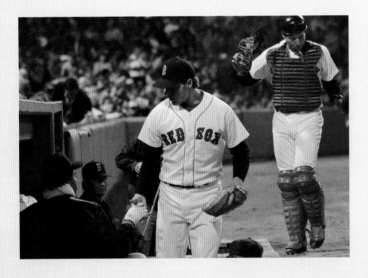 

He has done it twice, so in an odd way Clemens took the luster off his own accomplishment by being almost too dominant. But the first time for something always seems more special, and so it was on April 29, 1986 when the Fenway faithful were treated to a pitching performance that had never been seen previously. Clemens had almost unhittable stuff that Tuesday evening as he struck out 20 Seattle Mariners by throwing 70 percent of his pitches for strikes. The former record for strikeouts in a nine-inning game was 19; Clemens surpassed that number with a ninth-inning K of Phil Bradley. Clemens threw most of his 138 pitches in the mid-90 mph range; 97 were strikes and only 10 were put in play. The sparse crowd of 13,414 witnessed perhaps the most dominant performance ever by a pitcher. "The people who were here tonight saw history that won't be broken," said Gorman Thomas of the Mariners. "When the last out was made, I wanted to tip my cap. He was that good. It's the finest effort you'll ever see." Said Red Sox manager John McNamara: "I watched perfect games by Catfish Hunter and Mike Witt, but this was the most awesome pitching I've ever seen." Clemens duplicated the feat 10 years later in Detroit on September 18, 1996.

CARL YASTRZEMSKI'S FINAL WEEKEND

OCTOBER 1-2, 1983

THE NUMBERS, AMASSED DURING A GLORIOUSLY COMPETITIVE ERA FOR BASEBALL, WERE PHENOMENAL: 3,419 HITS, 452 HOME RUNS, 1,844 RBI, AND A 14-GAME WORLD SERIES BATTING AVERAGE OF .352.

Carl Yastrzemski stood in the shadow of the great Wall at Fenway for more than 20 years. That alone makes him royalty from Bangor to Bridgeport and everywhere in between. That he played the game with a hard-nosed style and a purpose in his pose, makes the events of October's first weekend in 1983 all the more poignant. "New England, I love you," Yastrzemski said.

It was "Yaz Day" and Fenway was aglow in the celebration of a man who won three batting championships, as well as the MVP Award during the "Impossible Dream" season of 1967. When Ted Williams faded away and Yaz came into focus in the early 1960s, the expectations for young Yaz were enormous. By this weekend in the early 1980s, he had surpassed all those expectations. The numbers,

amassed during a gloriously competitive era for baseball, were phenomenal: 3,419 hits, 452 home runs, 1,844 RBI, and a 14-game World Series batting average of .352.

The cheers on Yaz Day were deafening, not to mention a bit startling because of a deplorable season the Red Sox were enduring. But this wasn't for the team; this was for Yaz. Lasting, fervent applause continued and continued as Yaz was presented with material gifts and heartfelt testimonials. His words were brief and meaningful, but nowhere near as poignant as his lap around Fenway.

"I wanted to show my emotions," he said later. "For 23 years I always blocked everything out. I wanted to show these people that deep down, I was emotional for all that time."

NOMAR GARCIAPARRA'S RETURN

JULY 29, 2001

BEFORE THE DAY WAS OVER, GARCIAPARRA WOULD DELIVER A HOME RUN AND A TWO-RUN SINGLE — THE STUFF OF WHICH LEGENDS ARE MADE.

Folks in New England couldn't decide which happening was more incredible: The injury-riddled Red Sox staying within striking distance of a playoff berth midway through the 2001 season, or shortstop Nomar Garciaparra back in the lineup less than four months after undergoing delicate wrist surgery. On a glorious Sunday afternoon at Fenway Park, Sox fans greeted Garciaparra with a rousing ovation when he stepped into the box for his first at-bat of the season. Before the day was over, Garciaparra would deliver a game-tying home run in the sixth inning and a two-out two-run single in the seventh that won the game 4-3 — the stuff of which legends are made. "First game back — homer to straight-away center and a two-out base hit when we needed it. Kind of special," said Red Sox manager Jimy Williams. Added Red Sox pitcher David Cone: "Today gave Boston fans hope — hope that we're gonna give them something special down the stretch. "The ever-so-modest Garciaparra said. "It wasn't just me today; it was everybody. "But New England knew better; the Red Sox had climbed on Garciaparra's sturdy back and now it was up to him to carry them.

WHO COULD FORGET...

For every Ted Williams or Carl Yastrzemski who graces Fenway Park with a Cooperstown-caliber tool kit, the Red Sox produce a dozen loose screws and wing nuts of assorted shapes and sizes. Free spirits are a staple in team photographs, in grainy black-and-white and in vivid color. They permeate the atmosphere on Yawkey Way, like peanut vendors with operatic pipes.

You can look it up. From Babe Ruth's calorie-busting rookie year in 1914 to Wade Boggs' chicken-fed mysticism 70 seasons later, the Boston organization has assembled a parade of mavericks that the corporate, image-conscious Yankees never could match. Once you have seen Jimmy Piersall flap his arms like a seal or heard the story of Gene Conley trying to hop a flight to Jerusalem after a loss in New York, what Bronx tales can compare? Billy Martin and Reggie Jackson jawing in the dugout with neck veins bulging? Please. In Boston, it's more than permissible to scrap or speak out or stand apart from the crowd. It's a time-honored tradition.

From one decade to the next, through heart-rending finishes and the unyielding fatalism, Boston's oddballs and iconoclasts provided

WILLIAM FRANCIS LEE III

comic relief, pathos and great newspaper copy. They made rain delays bearable and the radio talk show telephone lines crackle with sheer outrageousness.

Some were Hall of Fame players; others lived on the fringe of the 25-man roster. Some displayed a pattern of aberrant behavior; others suffered from once-in-a-lifetime brainlock. Some bring a smile to the populace in hindsight; others will be remembered with a trace of sadness or regret. As a collection, they were the kids making faces in the Red Sox team picture.

Exhibit A: William Francis Lee III, who could have carved out a nice, comfortable place in Red Sox lore, instead of the parallel universe he seemingly inhabited, if only he were content to pipe down and change speeds with precision. The art of pitching came naturally

Offbeat characters are as integral to Red Sox tradition as Yankees-hating and second-guessing the manager. They drift on and off stage like the ensemble cast of "Seinfeld." Or in keeping with the Boston theme, "Cheers." There's Dick Stuart as Norm the roguish accountant, and Bernie Carbo as Woody the affable goofball. Sometimes the biggest challenge is keeping all the names and faces straight.

Babe Ruth, the quintessential cleanup man, bats leadoff in this particular order. Before Ruth broke home run

BABE RUTH

barriers and became a national treasure in New York, he was a crude rookie in Boston, so prone to spending money on women and drink that the Red Sox doled out his pay on a daily basis. Rooming with pitcher Ernie Shore as a rookie in 1914, Ruth borrowed his teammate's toothbrush. When Shore informed Ruth of that fact, the Babe replied, "That's all right. I'm not particular."

The 1930s brought intellectual catcher and future spy

MOE BERG

Moe Berg, of whom it was said, "He could speak seven languages and couldn't hit in any of them." Berg played with the Red Sox from 1935 through 1939. He contributed three home runs in that span and raised the collective clubhouse IQ by at least 50 points.

As a promising young outfielder with Boston in the early 1950s, Jimmy Piersall bowed after routine catches, once tormented pitcher Satchel Paige to the point of distraction and fought with everyone from Yankees second baseman Billy Martin to teammate Maury McDermott. Piersall underwent shock treatments at a state

MOE BERG [RIGHT]

MIKE GREENWELL

to Lee, and all the ingredients were in place for him to become his generation's answer to Mel Parnell, a lefty with the guts and gamesmanship to thrive in the unsettling shadow of the Green Monster. But the depth of Lee's perceptions set him apart from the cliche-spewing crowd. Forget his 94-68 record in a Red Sox uniform from 1969 through 1978. At his insightful best, he was more biting than a winter wind off the Charles River and loopier than a maze of rotaries.

In Boston, a city where the snowdrifts will obliterate a Volkswagen, Lee proved a single flake could make a difference. Teammate John Kennedy dropped the "Spaceman" label on Lee early in his career, and it followed him to Montreal, through retirement and into his second incarnation as a Zen Buddhist, Buckminster Fuller-quoting,

HAWK HARRELSON

subsistence farmer off the beaten track in Vermont. More than 20 years after leaving the Red Sox, Lee was traveling to Cuba for baseball exhibitions, catching fly balls behind his back, and dropping the name of Salem witch Lori Cabot into casual conversation. Other than that, he is just your standard retired jock.

It was former Brooklyn Dodgers great Duke Snider-we think-who once observed, "Bill Lee doesn't play with a full deck. But the cards he plays, he plays very well."

After the Red Sox sold his friend Bernie Carbo to the Cleveland Indians in 1978, Lee cleared out his locker in anger and bolted for a day. When general manager Haywood Sullivan fined him $533, Lee asked if the fine could be increased to $1,500 so he could take the entire weekend off.

Conversely, Lee was a baseball traditionalist who railed against artificial turf, the designated hitter and efforts to replace Fenway Park. He was an old-school competitor whose penchant for lipping off made others seethe. Lee might be the only player in baseball history who claims to have been sucker-punched by both a teammate (Reggie Smith) and an opponent (Mickey Rivers). Throw in the time Ellie Rodriguez's family attacked him in response to a confrontation in the Puerto Rico winter league, and Lee was 0 for 3.

While Lee's popularity blossomed over 10 years with the Red Sox, Ken "Hawk" Harrelson needed just a summer to put the entire city in

mental hospital in 1952, only to return and play 17 seasons in the big leagues.

Stuart, whose nickname was "Dr. Strangeglove," hit 75 homers and made 53 errors as Boston's first baseman in 1963 and 1964. With his awesome power, outsized ego and awful fielding, he inspired strong reactions pro and con. "Other ballplayers have loyal fans. I have loyal hecklers," Stuart told Sports Illustrated.

Gene Conley, a pitcher with the Red Sox and a forward for the NBA's Boston Celtics, played a starring role in one of the most bizarre incidents in club history. After taking an

JIMMY PIERSALL

early pounding in a 13-3 loss in New York on July 26, 1962, Conley drank several beers in the clubhouse. When Boston's team bus got stuck in traffic to the airport, a hot and agitated Conley hopped off for a bathroom break and took infielder Pumpsie Green with him.

When the traffic suddenly cleared, the two players were left behind in New York City. They dropped by Toots Shor's bar and spent the night at the Commodore Hotel. Green

GENE CONLEY

rejoined the Sox the following night in Washington, where he received a lecture and a $500 fine from manager Mike "Pinky" Higgins. Conley? He bought a plane ticket to Israel, with every intention of visiting the Promised Land. Problem was, he didn't have a passport, so he never made the trip.

Dick Radatz, a portrait in dominance for the Red Sox in the early 1960s, was renowned for striking out Mickey Mantle 47 times in 63 at-bats. After one such confrontation, Mantle unleashed a trail of obscenities and referred to Radatz as a "monster." When the outburst

HAWK HARRELSON   LUIS TIANT

his back pocket. The Red Sox signed Harrelson in 1967 after Kansas City owner Charlie Finley released him for popping off once too often. Harrelson played in 23 games for Boston's Impossible Dream team before busting loose for 35 homers and 109 RBIs in 1968. He quickly became a fan favorite in the guise of the Hawk, his nickname and alter ego.

"Pressure is the biggest killer of performance among athletes and in everyday life," Harrelson says. "That's the way I used to look at it-there was Ken Harrelson, and then there was the Hawk. If I was in the on-deck circle in a big game and there was a man on third base with one out, I'd say to myself, 'Kenny, get out of the Hawk's way and let him go.'"

Harrelson was a walking fashion statement as well as a revelation. His wardrobe won him a spot

HAWK HARRELSON

on America's top 10 best-dressed list. He wore gold medallions and bought a Nehru jacket of every color before they went out of style. In the quintessential act of cool, Harrelson defied old-school tradition and caught fly balls with one hand rather than two. The gesture typically would have infuriated Dick Williams, Boston's crusty manager. But

Williams let it slide. "I remember a writer asking why he allowed me to do it," Harrelson says. "Dick told him, 'If he keeps hitting home runs and driving in runs, I don't care what he does.'"

Although Harrelson made $50,000 in salary and even more in endorsements, he rarely paid for anything. In the Boston clubhouse, boxes of shirts and apparel routinely arrived from local clothiers for the Hawk; Harrelson would crack open the boxes and tell his teammates to take what they pleased. His popularity was such that he became one of the first professional athletes to hire a bodyguard for protection. He also retained an elderly gentleman named Wendell as his valet.

Harrelson couldn't muster the heart to say no to autograph seekers, so he would wait in the clubhouse for crowds to dissipate and still came out to find hundreds of fans waiting. He remembers walking into Jimmy's Harborside restaurant after a two-home run game and having the entire place rise en masse to give him a standing ovation.

When the Red Sox traded Harrelson to the Indians in 1969 for

DICK RADATZ

GEORGE SCOTT

resonated all the way to the press box, a classic nickname was born.

Radatz, who later became a radio talk show personality in Boston, recalls that a local paper sponsored a contest one summer in which fans were invited to pick a new name for him. "They came up with Smokey the Bear or some damn thing," Radatz says. "I said, 'Is that the best name you can come up with?' I told them we could stay with the Monster, because I had no problem with it. They said, 'We thought you didn't like it.' I told them, 'Nobody ever asked.'"

Luis Tiant, a man with a voice that approximated a Spanish dog whistle, roamed the Red Sox clubhouse from 1971 to 1978. Tiant routinely puffed on a cigar the size of a relay baton, and he dropped a trail of one-liners like a Cuban Johnny Appleseed. He would suck the stogie in the shower and the flame would never go out, a fitting metaphor for his career.

Tiant introduced a herky-jerky throwing motion that became the inspiration for pitchers from Fernando Valenzuela to Nuke LaLoosh. His genius for pitching was his

gift, and Red Sox fans applauded from the moment he began his walk from the bullpen.

Tiant was the rare player who knew when to apply the needle to restore equilibrium to a downbeat clubhouse. He would spot a pronounced physical trait in a teammate and pounce, calling Tommy Harper "Liver Lips" and Rico Petrocelli "Pinocchio." The humor wouldn't have resonated so deeply if Tiant didn't back it up with some of the most valiant pitching of his era.

George "Boomer" Scott, the pride of Greenville, Mississippi, sweated off pounds in a rubber suit and wore a

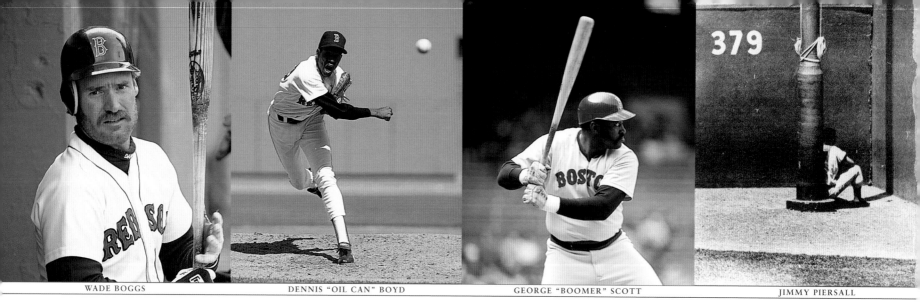

WADE BOGGS   DENNIS "OIL CAN" BOYD   GEORGE "BOOMER" SCOTT   JIMMY PIERSALL

Sonny Siebert, Vicente Romo and Joe Azcue, enraged fans picketed Fenway Park in protest, and a couple of local companies were sufficiently upset to cancel their season-ticket packages.

Like Harrelson, Dennis Boyd was a child of the South-namely Meridian, Mississippi, a textile and railroad center of 45,000 in the state's eastern hills. His boyhood friend Joe "Paps" Blanks christened him "Oil Can" because of his knack for consuming a heart-stopping brand of moonshine known as "oil."

Oil Can Boyd broke through as a big-time pitcher with Boston in 1985, winning 15 games and working 272 innings. He weighed 152 pounds, he says, with a brick in each pocket. If a pitch were invented, he'd throw it. And if it didn't exist, he'd invent it.

He celebrated strikeouts by pumping a fist in the air, patting teammates on their behinds, and sprinting to the dugout. At his childlike, ebullient best, he provided a refreshing dose of energy and innocence. "He was flamboyant — sort of like Dennis Rodman," says

DENNIS "OIL CAN" BOYD

Mike Easler, a member of the 1984 and 1985 Red Sox teams.

Boyd lacked Rodman's self-serving pretension. When he told stories of his mom and dad, Willie James and Sweetie Boyd, he wasn't lobbying for a movie deal. He spoke from the heart. And while Boston might have found Boyd's routine unsettling, there was more to the Can than a single snapshot could provide "I'm a historical type person," he says. "I knew about Plymouth and all the small towns. Sometimes I'd go to the symphony."

The Can was beguiling. One night in Cleveland, a fog rolled in so thick the players couldn't see their shoes, much less play baseball. Boyd told reporters, "That's what happens when you build a ballpark on the ocean."

The Can, the Hawk, the Spaceman and the Babe shared a similarly transcendent spirit, if not the same legacy. Their energy was too vibrant to corral and at times too complex to dissect. But the Red Sox were richer for it. And Fenway Park was a heck of a lot of fun when they were there.

Puka shell necklace that he claimed was made from second basemen's teeth. Scott endeared himself to fans by calling his home runs "taters" and showing cat-like ability at first base. During a tight pennant race, he summarized the sense of urgency by observing that the Yankees "are breathing down our throats."

Bernie Carbo, an outfielder with the Red Sox for five years in the 1970s, once gave an elderly gentleman in the clubhouse $10 to fetch him a cheeseburger and fries, only to later discover the old man was Red Sox owner Tom

BERNIE CARBO

Yawkey. Carbo even sat his stuffed gorilla, Mighty Joe Young, next to him on team flights. He also took the mascot into the clubhouse and occasionally carried the gorilla to restaurants for breakfast, all in the name of good luck.

During Mike Greenwell's 12 years with the Red Sox, fans sent him stuffed alligators in the mail in recognition of his alleged alligator wrestling. One year Greenwell wrestled with teammate Mo Vaughn during an argument at the

MIKE GREENWELL

batting cage. "I'm a four-wheel-drive pickup type of guy," Greenwell once told reporters. "So is my wife."

Wade Boggs, the poster boy for poultry consumption, made news for his finicky pre-game regimen. Boggs hurt his back taking off a pair of cowboy boots in his hotel room in Toronto, fell out of a vehicle driven by his wife when the passenger door flew open, and claimed to have willed himself invisible when a knife-brandishing mugger menaced him in Florida.